CHINESE BOXING AND KUNGFU

Written by Fan Tingqiang
Translated by Yang Daping
Illustrated by Li Zhaoqiu and Shi Lin

Shandong Friendship Press

First Edition 1998
ISBN 7—80551—987—0/G · 113

Published and Distributed by
Shandong Friendship Press
39 Shengli Street, Jinan, China
Printed by
Shandong Xinhua Printing House

FOREWORD

Boxing and Kungfu are like the two human legs. Either one without the other is inadequate in Wushu as is in walking. A cripple can hardly make fast, swift and flexible movements as fit people. This analogy claims that boxing learning has to go with Kungfu practice. Otherwise, the boxing may be eye-catching but impractical, and vice versa. Wushu experts often say, "Learning boxing without practicing Kungfu is bound to end up in vain while practicing Kungfu without learning boxing does not ensure any feats." They may also be analogized as hearing and sight, each is as important as the other. Having been engaged in Wushu for more than twenty years, Mr. Fan Tingqiang comprehends profoundly the gist of this philosophy of Wushu, to which "Chinese Boxing and Kungfu" provides a successful interpretation and helpful experiences.

Born into a family of Wushu, Tingqiang began learning Wushu when he was a little child. Before he joined the army, he had been apprenticed to Master Sufa, the famous martial monk of thirtieth descendant of Shaolin Temple, and learned Shaolin Boxing and weapons for eight years. Having obtained the authenticity from the master about the doctrine of Shaolin Boxing and a solid foundation of Chinese boxing and Kungfu, he is never complacent. During the two decades in the army, he always got up at three in the morning and went to Jinan Hero Hill to practice Wushu. Wearing a vest stuffed with fifteen kilos of iron grain, he jumped with double feet over the 177 steps from the bottom to the top of the hill and then, adjusting his breath for a moment, walked on hands down the hill. He did it to and fro for three times in order to gain strength of the limbs. Consecutively, he went forward with his boxing and Kungfu practice in the woods. In the evening, he would practice post and stake work for two hours before going to bed. And in daytime, he carried out his duties as a coach, training with the military guards. Day by day working hard like this, plus his merits and intelligence, enabled him to comprehend the gist of boxing and Kungfu quickly and make continual progress.

Tingqiang is a ambitious young man who is always ready to attain the highest realm of Wushu. Since he joined the army, he has been apprenticed to famous masters of Wushu, Li Zhanchen, Zhu Xianzhang, Sun Yujun and Yu Dongjin, to learn traditional feats of Baji, Shaolin, Xingyi, Bagua, Mantis and other boxing series, weapons, wrestling, and acu-point pressing respectively, in all of which he has tried his best and

1

constantly improved his skills.

Tingqiang has no sectarian bias. Whenever learning, he is modest in seeking the truth and doctrines and has greatest esteem for everyone who teaches him. He is tenacious in learning any boxing and Kungfu and never gives up. Wholly absorbed in Wushu, he has kept practicing everyday, summer or winter. Through more than twenty years' hard work of intensive training, he has obtained consummate skills of Wushu and has formed his own style by merging advantages of various schools of Wushu into one, which is a rare example for young learners.

In recent years, Tingqiang has passed his martial feats to young people either in the army or the localities and made such contributions in developing the cause of Chinese traditional Wushu, improving the combatant effectiveness of the army and maintaining the social security that he has been highly praised by the authorities and broad masses of people. His good deeds and achievements have been reported in many newspapers and books. Though he has won remarkable reputation, he has never been tempted by fame and wealth and, as always, he concentrates himself on Wushu. Making nothing of hardships, he wrote this book, "Chinese Boxing and Kungfu", which is composed of his knowledge and unique consciousness of Wushu.

Having read the book, I am deeply impressed by its specifications and illustrations of content, and its clarification and conciseness of writing. It provides the Wushu lovers and security personnel with a systematic, readable and operable textbook, a practical and comprehensive collection of skills and feats of Chinese boxing and Kungfu.

Niu Huailu

Shandong Academy of Wushu

Dec. 10, 1996

2

Content

Part One   General Exposition

Chapter One The outline of Chinese boxing and Kungfu

Section 1   Brief introduction of Chinese boxing and Kungfu

To facilitate the study of *Chinese Boxing and Kungfu*, it seems necessary to give the book a brief introduction.

Chinese Boxing and Kungfu divides into four parts as general exposition, Chinese boxing, Kungfu and annexes.

The first chapter of part one exposes the content of Chinese boxing and Kungfu and their relations, introduces the three steps in learning Chinese boxing and Kungfu, and expounds its uses and significance in modern times. The second chapter makes a classification of Kungfu, a study of strength, speed, pliability and the building of them, and an exposition of the distance, angle, timing and practical tactics in actual attack and defense of Chinese boxing and Kungfu.

Part two deals with Chinese boxing in which chapter one introduces systematically the variety of the performing styles and requirements of Shaolin Mantis Spreading Wings Boxing, emphasizing its special features in attack and defense. Chapter two of this part introduces the basic hand forms, hand work , step work and leg work. A complete series of Shaolin Mantis Spreading Wings Boxing is compiled in this chapter and each stroke and move of the boxing is well illustrated with figures and captions. Chapter three, through the illustration with figures and captions, demonstrates the functions and essentials of this boxing in actual combat.

Shaolin Mantis Spreading Wings Boxing, merging the four principal Chinese boxing styles into one, is a comprehensive style of Mantis boxing. It was passed by the master Yu Dongjin to only very few disciples and, therefore, it differs from other Mantis boxing series spreading in society. Master Yu often mentioned during his life time that he wound not pass the boxing to anyone other than his disciples and that once you learned this boxing you may dare to go anywhere alone in the world. He said he had been through all kinds of danger and hardship as a bodyguard in his early years and, combating against numerous master-hands with this boxing, he never lost. Obviously, Master Yu cherished this boxing dear. In order to carry on and enhance the Chinese martial art, enrich the physical culture of the people and for the purpose of body-strengthening and self-guard, the writer of this book, breaking through the superficial habit of keeping the secret from others, compiled the boxing series and made it public.

Part three: Kungfu. Chapter one introduces the essentials of Kungfu, elaborating the practical exercises, principles and warnings in training of both internal and external power. Illustrated figures and captions are added. The ten essential exercises in chapter two are results based on the writer's years of practicing and teaching. They have been proved rare know-how, easy to learn, fast in power developing and suitable for performers of all ages.

Part four consists of annexes of proverbs about Chinese boxing and Kungfu.

Section 2   Interpretation of Chinese boxing and Kungfu

Chinese Wushu is a national traditional item of physical training of attacking and defending skills, of which Chinese boxing and Kungfu are the major Components.

Chinese boxing is also called series, which is a composition of skills of hand work, eye work, step work, strength and spirit. It is a result of development of Wushu by certain historical stage.

The earliest record of complete formation of series appeared in Ming Dynasty, which already included the moving routs of active course and passive course and the records on main points, methods, verse of formulas, postures and specific requirements of hand work, eye work, body work, step work, strength, spirit and skills. The formation and perfection of the series have not only facilitated the teaching, watching, learning and exchanging of the art of Wushu, but also played a active role in the development, inheritance and innovation of the content of Wushu.

In the traditional Wushu, good boxing series requires not only reasonable compilation, solid content, but also the coherence of movements, variation and combination of attack and defense. In terms of pliability , speed and rhythm of strength, and the variation of hand work, body work and step work, the good series emphasize unique styles of different Wushu sects and cover as possible skills of Wushu, such as kicking, punching, throwing, grappling, stumbling and dropping.

In the training course of series, the hands should move along with the eyesight and the body work should coordinate with the step work. This is the technical requirement of "outer-three coordination and inner-three coordination"(nei san he and wai san he), which enhance the fully exertion of strength, skills and methods and the brimming with vigorous look and boldness of vision.

After practicing the series for a quite long period of time, the learner will be able to have a systematic mastery of the substances of Wushu and good development of hand work, eye work, body work, step work, strength, skills, good spiritual cultivation and improvement of Wushu quality, thus building a solid foundation for further learning of Wushu. Therefore, series have been strongly emphasized by the Wushu experts of all times and have become the compulsory courses of introduction and improvement of Wushu.

However, a good mastery of series does not necessarily mean the ability of winning in combat. What is indispensable is the Kungfu, including the internal work and external work.

The so called Kungfu here refers to the special techniques, with which the learner is to be trained intensively, systematically for a prolonged period of time with various modes. The training involves proper time (of Earthly Branches), place and *qigong* to develop both internal function and external function of the human body, which will enable the external body works in concert with the five internal organs and the six hollow organs (of Chinese Medicine) and thus building the body so strong as to have a enormous outer pounding power and a resistant power against pounding.

The pounding and anti-pounding power develops through the coordination of long time practice of breathing and special intensive training of pounding (with finger, palm, elbow, arm, shoulder, hip, knee, leg and feet) and anti-pounding (with head, chest, abdomen, rib, back and crotch). The internal human power will concentrate under the command of notion and burst out of certain part of the body.

The training of Kungfu takes a decisive position in Wushu practice. Without the various training of Kungfu, the boxing series will not function as expected. Sometimes, even if you hit the opponent with your skillful movements of series, you may be passive in fighting and finally beaten, because without Kungfu, your attack is weak and will contrarily expose your flaws to your opponent.

Only through long period of hard training of Kungfu and obtain a perfect mastery of it's feats, can you exert your boxing series skills and strength, and beat your opponent and protect yourself at the same time.

In addition, the training of Kungfu will improve your health, promote your vitality and prolong your life. Meanwhile, it helps cultivate your quality of wit, bravery and tenacity.

To sum up, boxing series and Kungfu are indispensable from each other. Series without Kungfu is yet good-looking but useless, while Kungfu without series is inflexible. Therefore, a Wushu learner must practice both boxing series and Kungfu as well as various weapons and other skills related to Wushu, in order to develop himself in a all-round way.

Section 3 Steps of practicing Chinese boxing and Kungfu

In learning Chinese boxing and Kungfu, whether in each posture, combination, simulated combat or in each step of Kungfu training, a regulation of steps and stages must be followed. Even if the learner has learned all the essentials and skills, he can not yet be able to put them into real combat until he completes the further practice "simulated combat".

1. "Learning" period

Through detailed reading and study of the illustration, a learner can get to know the specifications of the movements such as hand posture, step posture, body posture and the routes of movements. For a new learner, it is better to have one or more colleagues to work together, so that one may correct the other's movements according to the illustration of the book. However, when one is learning alone, he may work in front of a big mirror, to see if his movements are standard. At the beginning, one should not hurry to seek for speed and strength, but concentrate on regulation of the specifications. The speed and strength should be added gradually when one's movements meet the requirements. However, one should exert his strength in compliance with his own physical characters and the natural movement of his muscles and joints so as not to build incorrect moving patterns and affect his further learning. After practicing for a period of time, one may work for sections of movements and then for series. Cohesion should be emphasized as well as regulations.

A unity of outer work of hands, eyes, body, steps and the inner work of spirit, breathing, strength and power should be realized. At the same time, comparing with the illustrated figures of simulated combat, one may learn the usage of the movements in actual combat and, thereby, one's interests of training will be enhanced and training quality improved.

2. "Simulated combat" training

By the time one has got a grasp of rather proficient and regular series as well as the connotations of attack and defense of each movement and, also, he has got certain background of Kungfu, he should begin the next stage of training, "simulated combat", which is the only way one proceeds to actual combat from series training and is a efficient way of improving one's attacking and defending ability of Chinese boxing and Kungfu. It is a simulated combat by two learners, one of whom is a imaginary enemy. By "simulated combat" practice one is able to obtain a deeper comprehension of the skills of the series, get a feeling of the change of the component's strength, and find out

4

the attacking distance, angle and the flaws and vulnerable points of the component. The one playing the feeding part in "simulated combat" may change his pliability of speed and strength, adjust his angle and add certain resistance according to the conditions of the practicing part, so as to increase the intensity of the "simulated combat", transferring to actual combat. Nevertheless, "simulated combat" is not actual combat anyway. For the sake of safety, the speed, strength and attacking points are controlled in a limit. The human instinct and initiative can not be inspired as in actual combat to beat the enemy even with one ruthless movement. Therefore, the compensation is to practice through apparatus beating, "empty beating" or "notional boxing". For instance, imagine an enemy attacks you from certain direction and you react immediately with responding movements to beat the attacker ruthlessly. You should simulate the place, postures, intention and other related factors of the enemy and should concentrate your attention on performing the movements with high quality. By "beating the figure or his shadow", you can build an instinct response of attack and defense, and thus, you are able to improve your power to deal with an emergency and fully exert your fighting potential in actual combat.

3. Actual combat of attack and defense

Apart from strengthening physiques and keeping fit, the major purpose of practicing Chinese boxing and Kungfu is actual combat of attack and defense. Actual combat differs from "simulated combat", in which the conditions are ever changing, opponents different, hardship and dangers unpredictable, and winning opportunities fleeting. Therefore, the boxer is required, in whatever complex situation, to be calm, brave and flexible, beating the enemy with efficient skills and tactics.

Section 4　Uses and significance of practicing Chinese boxing and Kungfu

1. Strengthening physique, keeping fit and self-defense

An obvious effect of practicing Chinese boxing and Kungfu is in strengthening one's physique against diseases and keeping fit. As a traditional exercise and sport, Wushu has been greatly influenced by medicine during its development and, therefore, is of great value in keeping fit and in medical treatment. Nowadays, some boxing series as well as *qigong* has been used widely in clinical practice, effective in strengthening physique, adjusting psychology and curing and preventing diseases. Among them, a typical example is the popular *taijiquan*.

In the practice of Chinese boxing and Kungfu, it is usually required to "combine spirit with form", i. e., to instruct the body moving by spirits, so as to strengthen the body and vitalize the spirit. For internal work in particular, the function of "notion" is emphasized on the training of "spirit." The highly harmonious unity of human shape and internal notion plus rhythmical breathing will not only function on the brain work, but also provide positive training to central nervous system. In addition, the vitality cultivated in practice of Chinese boxing and *qigong* will help prolong human life.

Another distinct effect of Chinese boxing and Kungfu is self-defense. The boxing and Kungfu is centered with attack and defense while its existence and development are based on the functions of self-defense and vanquishing the enemy. A long-term training will enable one to have a mastery of various skills of attack and defense and an ability of combating, so as to help in keeping social security, protecting human rights, defending oneself and conquering the enemy.

2. Tempering willpower and cultivating moral character

Practicing Chinese boxing and Kungfu may temper one's willpower and cultivate good qualities of endurance, bravery and wisdom.

The endurance of hard work is of primary importance in practicing Chinese boxing and Kungfu. In particular, the training of Kungfu requires hardworking even more. When practicing stake work, for instance, one has to overcome the barriers of aching and swelling muscles. When training with the Ten Essential Works, one will overcome not only the barriers of aching muscles and skeleton, but also barriers of cold and hot weather. It is necessary to keep up a long term training of Chinese boxing and Kungfu. And a fixed time and place for the practice is preferred. Perseverance is required and laziness must be overcome, and so must all kinds of barriers occurring in life. In a word, there are always various factors in reality which will condition you and affect your practicing boxing and Kungfu. If you don't have strong willpower and endurance of hardship, it is very difficult for you to persevere and you may even give up halfway. It is clear that the course of improving your boxing and Kungfu is one in which you work hard and temper your will.

During the course of practicing boxing and Kungfu, you may form a broad mind and a noble morality of Wushu. The adherents of Wushu cherish their teachers and colleagues, think highly of courtesy and friendship, and never take advantage of their power and feat to bully people. Their practice of drilling and combat cultivate their wit, bravery and boldness, while the practice of internal exercise help to keep oneself calm and in a good mood and thereby to conserve morality and sentiment.

3. Studying and comprehending the gist of the national culture and thoughts

Wushu has close relations with the Chinese ancient philosophy, military affairs and arts. Therefore, we may learn much about the gist of the national culture and thoughts as we learn Chinese boxing and Kungfu. In the field of Wushu there is a wide-spread saying "Boxing initiated from *yi* (*I Ching*) and its theory consists of medicine", which highly summarizes the close relation of the development of Wushu with the *yi* , the gist of Chinese ancient philosophy.

The thought of *yi* holds that the human body is a small universe while the nature is a big one. The small universe responds the big universe as the human being is an outcome of the nature. And human being cannot do without the environmental conditions provided by the "earth and heaven". This is the thought of "heaven and human being respond each other" and "heaven and human being form a unity of one". This thought has been realized in the training of Chinese boxing and Kungfu as the requirements of training time and place, such as "To train in *sanjiu* (of Chinese calendar) in winter and *sanfu* (of Chinese calendar) in summer" and *Zishigong* "which is practiced in *zishi* (midnight). According to traditional Chinese medicine, *zishi* is the hour when "Yang" initiates. Practicing at this time will get double achievement with half the effort. In general, the practice should be conducted in accordance with the inner relation of natural chronology and environment with the human viscera. It should also follow the changing rules of *Yin and Yang*.

Taijiquan, which is well-known nowadays, has been developed on the basis of the theory of five circuit phases and six atmospheric influences of Chinese medicine, and the thought of the relative waxing and waning of *Yin and yang*. *Taiji*, the word itself is from "*Zhou Yi - Xi Ci Shang*, "which reads, "*Yi* has *Taiji* which consists of two opposites. " It reflects a level of the developing matter and this level is in a critical state of which the *Yin and Yang* haven't been decided. From the view of the moving mode of matter, it is a mobile state without shape. In boxing, it is performed as the breathing exercise and the transformation between movement and stillness, toughness and pliability, emptiness and solidness, and opening and closing.

Bagua Zhang (*Eight Diagrams* boxing) is actually deduced from the Bagua thinking of "*Zhou Yi*". The regulations and systems of Bagua boxing are consistent to the theory of Bagua and based on the instructions of the principles of *Yi* .

Xingyi Boxing is indispensable from the ancient theory of "*Five Elements*. " Besides, Xingyi Boxing has a deep relation of origin with the Chinese traditional Confucianism. The movements of Xingyi are simple, changes are succinct and steps pithy and, after all, functional. The structure of body positions are basically the style of *sancai* (the Three Geniuses of Taoism : the heaven, the earth and the man) , with which one holds in harmony. When performing, your arms and elbows are half bending and half holding out as if attacking but reserved. All these characters of the boxing realize the manner of Confucianism, emphasizing on pragmatism and the doctrine of the *mean*.

In brief, the origin and development of Chinese Wushu has indispensable relations with the Chinese ancient philosophies. Some Wushu sects are named after the subject titles of Chinese ancient philosophies and hold the principles of them as their instruction. Therefore, at the same time when we learn the Chinese boxing and Kungfu, we may also study the quintessence of the Chinese ancient philosophies, the function of which should not be ignored.

4. Benefiting the construction of ideological civilization and the cultural exchange with other peoples

Wushu is an excellent cultural heritage of the Chinese nationality. In addition to its functions of strengthening physique and self-defense, it has high value of performance, appreciation and recreation. The boxing series, weapon performance, free sparring and *qigong* performance are popular events. The extensive development of Wushu may purify the general mood of the society, enrich and activize the people's ideological and cultural life and benefit the construction of ideological civilization. Besides, the expansion of the exchanges of Wushu with foreign countries may not only increase the mutual understanding and friendly communication between the peoples, but also help China to expand economic exchanges with other countries and promote China's economy.

Chapter Two   An initial exploration of theories of Chinese Boxing and Kungfu

Section 1   Classification of Kungfu

The so-called soft work, hard work, internal work and external work are classified at different angles. There are disputes on the expositions of the classification of Wushu. By my viewpoints and in compliance with those familiar to people, I made my classification as follows:

1. From a view of function, effect and purpose, Kungfu divides into two classes : pounding-attack and pounding-resistance

Pounding-attack is for the purpose of beating and winning the enemy. This Kungfu is trained through the coordination of inner vitality and outer human power to conduct long-term exercises of pounding with certain parts of the body so as to strengthen the attacking function and power. Examples are the training work exposed in this book, such as head work, fist work, finger and palm work, elbow work, knee work, foot work, etc.

Pounding-resistance is obviously a reactive feat of Kungfu. It also requires long-term exercise of inner vitality and outer pounding on certain parts of the body so as to enable the learner to stand being pounded that ordinary people are not able to. Examples of the feat exposed in this book are head work, arm work, breast-back work and rib-abdomen work.

2. From a view of strength and performance, Kungfu divides as soft work and tough work

Soft work, also called *Yinshougong* , is a hidden power. Take *Shaolin Yangguang-shou as* an example. When training, a candle or incense will be lit and put on the table in a completely dark room. Stand in horse-riding stance, keep *qi* (vitality) at *dantian* (the pubic region), concentrate on the light of the candle and pound it with your fist or palm in a distance which is made farther gradually. Until you are able to hit the light out from distance, you succeed. With this Kungfu you can attack the enemy's heart and other inner organs from distance.

However, it is difficult to succeed in this Kungfu, because of its extremely strict requirements of the background and time. In fact, few people succeed because it takes a much longer period of time. The elementary success takes 3-5 year and the higher level takes 10-20 years, which is beyond ordinary people. Therefore, the learner should start from childhood and keep perseverance.

Tough work, compared with soft work, is so called. It is the work in which a combination of inner *qi* and outer power is built to pound fatally or resist attacks safely with limbs, head, breast, back, ribs and abdomen. The work will make one strong both inside and outside with good elasticity to fit the pounding and resistance.

In training of tough work one must follow in order and progress step by step, from light to heavy, slow to fast, and must keep on practice according to qualities and conditions. Nevertheless, compared with soft work, tough work is easier in terms of time it takes and restraints it requires.

3. From a view of emphasis, Kungfu divides into internal work and external

Internal work emphasizes on training of the interior function of the body (notion, breath and qi, viscera, acupuncture channels, blood passages etc.), while external work emphasizes on training of exterior body parts such as skin, bones and muscles.

In a word, regardless of initiative pounding or pounding-resistance, soft work or tough work, internal work or external work, they are only classifications made from different angles of view without much essential distinction. None of them will do without the three essentials as notion, vitality and strength. The aim of their cultivation is vitality, and their training principles are the same. Therefore, the learner should not emphasize one thing at the expense of another. Further more, Kungfu should be practiced along with the skills of boxing series, to make progress in a down-to-earth manner.

Section 2　Speed and pliability in Chinese boxing and Kungfu

The highest realm of Chinese boxing and Kungfu skills are realized in actual combat, in which one changes his strength constantly according to the opponent's changes of speed and pliability of attacking. One may conquer the tough with softness, the slow with speeding, with flexibility and merging of softness and firmness, to win the combats accordingly. However, this superior level of skills can not be acquired in a short time. It needs but a prolonged period of time of hard work with wisdom, plus the instruction of good masters.

In the elementary stage of training, in order to obtain a good grasp of essentials of the boxing skills, the learner must relax his body, slow down his movements, make a careful study of the structure of the movements and see to it that his hands, eyes, head, shoulder, waist, legs and lower body are in good harmony. Never be anxious to get fulfilled. Having learned the essentials of movements in a while, the learner move into the

10

stage of strength training, in which fastness and sudden force is the key. When one feels trained and regulated, back to slow and soft training again, exercising slowly and smoothly like doing Taijiquan. At this stage, one must try to feel the moving of his hands, eyes, body, steps, the changing of his muscles, skeleton in movements and the flowing and circulation of blood and *qi*. After training like this for a while, go back to tough training again, to sense the fastness and sudden force. And then, after certain time, slow down again. Step by step and day after day, the learner progresses in a spiral way up until he moves as fast as a barrow when attacking and as nimble as an ape when defending.

One thing has to be clear that when training to be tough, one should not have strained muscles, clenched teeth, wide-opened eyes, suffocated breath and stiff joints, but be calm and natural, fast and smooth, firm and flexible at the same time. He should always maintain his normal physiological condition and natural muscles and joints.

On the other hand, the training of softness dose not mean loose. Rather, it requires the learner to be calm and flexible, outwardly soft but inwardly tough. The movements must be performed in curve routes and in good cohesion and coordination. Though the performer seems slow and gentle, he is always ready to be fast and aggressive in actual combat.

Besides, when training speed and pliability, one's breathing adjustment must be harmonious with movements, inhaling when withdrawing and exhaling when attacking. The strength and speed is also adjusted through breathing. In slow and soft training, the breathing must be smooth like flowing water yet very brief and heavy in fast and forceful training. So, the adjustment of breathing in the training of speed and pliability is an important link that must not be ignored.

After the above mentioned repeated training and when one has got a intimate knowledge of speed and pliability, his next training is conducted through the two-men-work, practising with his master. He studies the changes of strength, speed and pliability in combat, finding out the strength points, opportunities and angles so as to improve his ability of flexible defense and fast attack. In this training one moves according to the partner's (supposed opponent's) ever changing of strength, speed and pliability. Nevertheless, in the contest between master-hands, transformation of softness and firmness is difficult to tell. It changes in accordance with the opponent's strength without marks. It occurs beyond thinking of the variation of simultaneous conditions.

Section 3　Strength in Chinese boxing and Kungfu

As we all know, the weight lifters are usually so strong that they can easily lift a heavy barbell overhead. However, it is difficult for them to perform a movement of deep-knee bending or fist pushing. Their movements are stiff with little pounding power and they are sweating and out of breath in movements. It is not that they do not have strength, but that they do not have a mastery of the skills of how to exert their strength. From this, we can see that the so called "force" in Chinese boxing and Kungfu differs significantly and conceptually from the common strength.

Force is crucial to the practice of Chinese boxing and Kungfu, for it is one of the major indices of the level of one's Kungfu.

1. Developing absolute strength

The outcome of force is based on the absolute strength of the human body. It is a "vital strength" transformed from human strength through special training. Therefore, one needs to develop absolute strength in order to have the explosive force in Chinese boxing and Kungfu. The training of absolute strength may be carried out by various methods and with apparatus such as barbell, dumbbell and combined apparatus. Push-up, hand-stand or hand-walk are also helpful. You may arrange to do the Push-up on the basis of your own conditions. Beginners may do it by progressive decrease as to do 12 for the first time, 9 for the second time and 5 to 6 for the third time. After training for a period of time, it should be carried out by progressive increase, say, 6 for the first time, 9 for the second time and 12 for the third time until up to hundreds of times in one training time. The methods of progressive decrease and increase not only do good to one's absolute strength stamina, but also help improve his vital capacity. In doing push-up, inhale smoothly when letting the body downward, and, when lungs are full, making a pause, push suddenly and puff to exhale. To add your training intensity, many other exercises of weight loading may be adopted.

2. Enforcing the training of pliability

You may feel, after training of absolute strength for a while, that your muscles are stout and joints solid but lack explosive force and speed. Then, how to turn your strength into force?

First, the training of body pliability must be enforced when absolute strength is being acquired. As we know, the dumpling-shaped muscles are powerful and explosive yet they are poor in endurance, while the strip-shaped muscles have not only power and endurance, but also good tenacity and greater scope of movement. The training of pliability helps to turn the dumpling-shaped muscles into strip-shaped muscles and stretch the joints so that the whole body becomes flexible to exert force.

Second, it's helpful to train in strength-speed. A valid exercise of the training is that, at the intervals of the absolute strength training, do some relaxing movements and then push forward fast or perform other skills with speed.

The exercises in training of speed and pliability in boxing series, with firmness and softness in harmony, are also helpful to improve the techniques of force exertion.

3. Enforcing the training of "tranquil force"

The training of "tranquil force" is an effective way of developing stamina and adjusting the balance of the force of the upper and lover body. Take stake work as an example. Once the gravity center of the body is stable, all the parts of the body will be in a state of balance. With this balance and the adjustment of consciousness, the force, which is a balance of all directions and all levels, will be turned out. Another example is the Horse-riding stance stake work in which the learner keeps half squatting, so as to improve the strength stamina and facilitate the superior unity of the inner factor (vitality) and the outer factors (the hands, eyes and body).

4. Enforcing the training of the waist

Normally, the force of Chinese boxing is initiated from the lower limbs and reaches to the four ends (the hands and the feet) by the function of the waist. Waist is called in traditional Wushu the "middle joint" for it is the axis of the lower and upper parts of the body. Only if the "middle joint" is flexible, harmonious and vigorous, can the initiative power of the legs be transferred to the "tip ends" so as to exert full, focusing, explosive and flexible force. Masters of Wushu have emphasized that "He who learns boxing without training of his waist will not be a master."

There are various methods of waist exercises to improve the flexibility, elasticity and controlling ability of the ligament and muscles of one's waist. In order to fully exert the force in boxing, the alternation of the muscles should be realized, i.e., the muscles must work as contraction muscles and dilators alternatively in the exertion of the force. In addition, the force should be initiated from the mid-line of the body so that the force of the whole body can be collected and put into one point, plus the acceleration made when the force approaches the target, a even more explosive power being acquired.

Section 4 Distance, angles and timing in Chinese boxing and Kungfu in actual combat

1. Distance

In the actual combat, the two opponents. are often in a state of watching each other, keeping a distance from each other. Anyone who is attacking has to approach the rival with quicksteps; similarly, the defender has to step back quickly to keep the distance to avoid being hit.

The distance between the two opponents before they come to grapples is usually kept:

a) in a distance of one or two arm-length. Within this distance, you are able to get the rival with just a body-turning.

b) in a distance of two steps, within which you must make one forward-step before you turn your body and initiate the attack.

In the actual combat, the adjustment of distance is made mainly by stepping forward and backward or moving left and right. The speed and length of the stepping will effect the attack and defense directly. On one hand, you must moving and changing your steps flexibly so as to make it difficult for the opponent to get the fight attacking distance, and , on the other hand, you must approach or dodge your opponent in swift movement. For example, when you cannot dodge the opponent's quick attack in time, you may meet head-on. Stagger his moving direction and step forward instead. In this way, you destroy his effective attacking distance and approach him at the same time so that you may pound him with your body or joints, or hit the vital parts of his body with touching force.

2. Angles

The angles in actual combat refer to the angles made by the defending postures, forwarding directions and attacking directions of the limbs between the two opponents.

It is common to change the attacking and defending angles through the movement of steps and transformations of the body position. Take the movement of "right parrying-block" of Mantis Spreading Wings Boxing as an example. When the opponent is pounding your face with his right fist, you step forward with left foot to his right side to stagger his attacking direction and, with the twisting force of your waist to the right, you parry and block his right arm right-backward and downward to change his attacking angle and force direction. Commonly-used moving steps are slanting step, horizontal step and zigzag step.

Another usage is the out-flanking tactics to avoid front punching and attack sideward at the same time. Examples are the movements of the cycling walk in Bagua Zhang or the left and right star-picking Bagua step.

3. Timing

In addition to the adjustment of effective distance and creation to advantageous angles, time is also crucial in beating the enemy in actual fighting.

Example one: When the opponent is pounding in your face with his right hand, you avoid it by turning your body. Next, he must get back his arm and you should take this opportunity, stepping forward with your left foot, and hit his face with a left swing.

Example two: When the opponent kicks your private part (the crotch) with right foot, you slip half a step, with your body turning left, and lift left foot to parry his right foot and kick his left knee simultaneously.

In general, you must take the opportunities of attacking and defending at the right moments. Early movement may expose your intention to the opponent so that he may change his movement, while late movement may leave him opportunities to hit you. Therefore, you should have good reaction to meet the requirement as you stand still if the enemy is not moving; but "you initiate the movement prior to his moving."

Section 5 Practical tactics in Chinese boxing and Kungfu

Ever since the ancient times, the military leaders have won their battles and wars on the bases of their strategies and tactics, and so have the masters of Wushu.

1. Tactics adopted on different enemies

A) To combat the rival who is shorter than you

The short person normally has a lower and steady center of gravity, who is usually quick in movement and has explosive strength and flexible targets in attacking. Once he gets the advantages he is able to push the rival double of his weight meters away from him. The short person prefers close combat so that he can hit the rival on the vital parts such as the crotch, ribs etc.

To combat the shorter opponent, you must keep certain distance from him. Half length of your height is preferred. Your steps must be simple and quick, never in cross-step or low empty-step which may leave opportunities for the opponent to attack. Face the opponent with "side horse-riding stance." Keep moving your hands according to your feet movements and keep your arms half bent. Try not to make movements in the air or in single-leg stance but stand steadily and collect your body to save power. Never initiate to attack but wait at your ease for an exhausted enemy.

B) When fighting against a rival who is bigger, you must be clear that he may make distant attack for his longer limbs but he may be slow and inflexible for his high center of gravity. To combat this kind of enemy, importance should be attached to some aspects. First, attack his lower parts such as crotch and chest sides region, taking advantage of your shorter figure, and force him to bend and become passive. Second, attack him simultaneously when he withdraws, for the taller is usually slower, Third, use outflanking tactics and attack him from the flank by your foot moving and body turning. And fourth, attack him by changing your targets—hit his lower parts first and, when he bends to protect them, hit his head instead. Hit him on the breast to make him back-bending and change your targets to his private parts and chest sides region.

C) Combating between the old and the young

The elder opponent usually lacks stamina and strength but has more experience and solid Kungfu. Therefore, when fighting against the young rival, he should be steady and waits at ease for the young one to get exhausted. The young one is normally swift, strong with better stamina, but he is often anxious to win and apt to be taken in by the old one's tricks. So in the actual combat, the young one must try to keep calm and make use of his superiority of energy and speed, to interfere the old one's position and finally to win.

2. Making use of the terrain

Advantageous terrain is an important condition in actual combat in Wushu as is in military battles. Some specific applications of terrain are as follows:

A) In hillside fields, try to occupy the upland; on the slopes, try to get to the comparatively flat spot; use the trees for protection if possible.

B) In the water of water fields, try to take the flat spot with shallow water.

C) On the road, try to occupy the wider section; and make use of the available objects for defense.

D) In a lane, try to get the spot with fewer people but make use of the people and the objects for protection.

E) In a coach, try to get at the window or the door and use the handrail for protection.

F) In a room, try to occupy the window, the door or the corner of the walls, which make it easy to retreat and to prevent the enemy attacking from flank.

G) In the stairs, try to get the landings, turnings and the up part of the handrails.

To sum up, one should decide his position in combat according to the specific conditions of the terrain and keep clear-minded to make the best use of the objects at his side to facilitate the final winning.

3. To forestall the enemy or strike only after the enemy

To forestall the enemy is based on your good knowledge and judgment of the enemy and the conditions of the combat, with which you can seize the opportunity and beat the enemy with one strike. Otherwise, you may keep steady and wait at ease and to strike only after your enemy. It all depends on the specific circumstances.

A) When the enemy is found poor at Kungfu, or slow in reaction or in low spirits, you can take the chance and forestall him.

B) When the enemy is in passive state or careless and mind-distracted, forestall him.

C) Having found out the enemy is unskilled except his big figure, forestall him.

D) when the two rivals are of the same level of Wushu and Kungfu, the one who is bigger may initiate the strike.

E) When you know the enemy's skills at your fingertips, you can forestall him.

F) When you have learned that the enemy's Kungfu is higher than yours, you must keep distance from him and wait for opportunities to strike only after him.

G) When you are not clear about the actual strength of the enemy and have no certainty of success, you can strike after him.

H) When you have learned that the opponent is a master-hand, you must not strike before he does.

I) When combating a mysterious opponent, strike only after him.

J) When a senior combating a junior, the senior usually strikes only after the junior.

K) When a master of superb skills and noble morality of Wushu combating one of less skills and morality, the former usually strike after the latter.

4. Using solidness and emptiness in alternation

There is no stable methods and manipulations in using military forces but alterations according to the circumstances of the enemy, dodging its strong points and attacking its weakness. In actual combat of Wushu, the alteration of attacks and feints is also adopted to deal with various enemies.

When the opponent neglects defense or lacks force, you can come straight to the point and beat him with firmness. But when you are at the same level of power with the opponent, there is no certainty of your winning. Then you can use feints to interfere the opponent and break his defense and, finally, you turn feints into actual attack and beat the opponent with a sudden movement.

Suppose you are pounding the opponent on his face with straight right blow and he is turning his head leftward to dodge. Then you should turn your straight blow into right swing to hit him on the left side of his head. Here, your straight blow is a feint and your swing is solid. This is an example in the movement.

In the aspect of force, the transformation of softness and firmness is often realized. A movement may look firm but is soft or vise versa, it is changing all the time.

Although the transformation of softness and firmness seems changeable, it has its own rules as the transformation of *the five elements (metal, wood, water, fire and earth* of Chinese medicine)*, which should be adopted according to circumstances.

Part Two   The boxing
Chapter One   The unique Shaolin Mantis Spreading Wings Boxing

Section 1   The origin of Shaolin Mantis Spreading Wings Boxing

The former name of Shaolin Mantis Spreading Wings Boxing was "Shaolin Taiji Bagua Mantis Boxing." According to the legend, long time ago in Shaolin temple there was a warrior monk of great attainments in both Wushu and Buddhism. He traveled all around the country and sought for studies. Wherever he learned about wonderful people, especially those excelled in Wushu and Kungfu, he would try every way to visit them and stay with them so that he could talk about Buddhist doctrines and allegories and exchange martial arts with them. He made many friends with wonderful people in the society of Wushu, yet with only three of whom hitting it off. The four of them agreed on that they meet on the Moon Festival every year. Many years later they met again as usual. After talking glowingly, the monk asked the other three to become monks like him and spend the rest of life in temples in the mountains to concentrate on Buddhism

and martial arts. But they refused to do so at last because they should not abandon their families. Having no alternatives, the monk put forward a suggestion. "We four of us are nearly sixty years old and it will be difficult for us to meet every year." he said, "Why don't we each contribute our feats to compile a style of boxing that we can practice after we go apart. That will be a good memento." The other three agreed with him whole-heartedly. So, one of them contributed skills of Taiji, one of Bagua and on of Mantis. The monk did that of Shaolin where he was from. They practiced together for several days until they were all contented. At the departure, the monk said, "I have no idea when shall we meet again, but I wish the Buddha will bless us all to attain much, and we will be like big birds to stretch our wings to fly high. So, let's call this boxing we founded "spreading wings boxing." They never met again afterwards. The monk, who resumed secular life later, kept on practice and improvement of the boxing and made more contributions to it, especially to those movements of Mantis, for which he had partiality.

Though Shaolin Mantis Spreading Wings Boxing is a result of friendship between the four of them, the warrior monk played the most important part in the making of it. Therefore, to commemorate him and, also to distinguish the boxing from other mantis boxing series, it has been named as "Shaolin Mantis Spreading Wings Boxing" or, simply, "Spreading Wings Boxing."

Section 2　The performing requirement of various styles of Shaolin Mantis Spreading Wings Boxing

Because Shaolin Mantis Spreading Wings Boxing is an assembly of skills of the four major boxing schools, it may be performed in the styles—— Taiji, Shaolin, Bagua and Mantis. In addition, this boxing is beyond the restrain of age. The young learners may do it with strength, while the old can perform it in a gentle course. The boxing is therefore superior in that it is beyond limitation of age to which many kinds of boxing are confined.

1. The performance of Taiji style

Shaolin Mantis Spreading Wings Boxing can be performed according to the requirement of performing Taiji in that the trunk of body must be upright and relaxed, your mind calm and concentrating. All movements are to be led by Yi and Qi. The breath must be smooth and combined naturally with movements which are gentle and spry. Your waist functions as a pivot to promote the limbs, the ends of which in turn to lead the body as a whole.

The movements are jointed harmoniously, speeding alternatively at intervals, soft when transforming and explosive when dropping. The two hands move as if holding a ball to make curve strokes. The force originates from the legs and waist, reaches to the arms and fingers, accumulates as if on a bowstring and bursts out like a barrow.

2. The performance of Shaolin style

According to the requirements of Shaolin Boxing, the movements of the series must be stretching and collecting generously and performed in straight routs. The force must be steady internally but forceful externally, speeding alternatively with clear rhythm. The step work consists mainly of bow stance and horse stance, steady in both offense and defense but bold and vigorous in attacking.

3. The performance of Bagua Zhang style

When performed according to the requirements of Bagua Zhang, all the hand forms must be in palm patterns, fingers being apart and palm hollow somewhat sunken. In the position, the front hand palm hollow is inward and back hand hollow downward.

The moving is basically in curving routs. When moving left, your left hand is put at the front and your right hand at the left elbow as protection, and vise versa.

The position also conforms to the requirements of Bagua Zhang with upright back, inward breast, collected bottom and Qi sunk in Dantian. In particular, the performance of Bagua Zhang should be natural and smooth like floating clouds and flowing water.

4. The performance of Mantis Boxing style

Mantis Boxing belongs to imitative boxing. It's famous in the world of Wushu for its interlocking movements and quick attacks. Shaolin Mantis Spreading Wings Boxing is of a style similar to Plum Taiji Mantis Boxing but superior to it in that the former is particular about the transformation of solidness and emptiness, softness and toughness, its movements being fast yet solid, and elaborated yet interlocked.

Section 3　The distinctive features of Shaolin Mantis Spreading Wings Boxing in attack and defense

Because Shaolin Mantis Spreading Wings Boxing has absorbed the essence of four major schools of Chinese boxing, it is distinct for its features in attack and defense.

1. On attacking routs

The boxing has adopted both the straight-in-stride character of Shaolin boxing and the circling-stride of Bagua

Zhang. In actual combat, therefore, one may use both alternatively according to various circumstances to ensure the initiative.

2. On attacking approaches

The attacking approaches of the boxing differ in a way from that of other schools. In either frontal attack or flank attack, if left foot is ahead, the attack is to be initiated by the left parts and limbs of the body; if right foot is ahead, one attacks with his right limbs and body parts. In this way, one can approach his opponent at possibly nearest distance and, meantime, keep the harmony of his body as a whole.

3. On hand skills and defense

The boxing has adopted the feature of hand skills of Taiji Boxing in that the two hands move as if holding a ball, rolling forward when you advance and inward when you retreat. You keep your two hands always before your breast, with one hand ahead aiming at the opponent's throat and the other behind protesting your Huagai point and aiming at the part below his Huagai point. The two hands transfer each other to coordinate in attacking and defending. The defence of this boxing is mid-line principled, which keeps the nearest distance for defense and possibly minimum extent of body turning to make the attack and defense almost at the same time. If you are attacked from the right, turn left to dodge and attack back with your left hand

and left foot. If attacked from the left, turn right to dodge and attack back with your right limbs.

4. On steps

In stepping, the boxing requires that the forward foot touches the ground with the complete sole while the hind foot only with the front part of the sole. When advancing, the hind foot follows the forward foot and, when retreating, the feet slip back. When moving crosswise, the hind foot also keeps following the forward foot so as to keep the body steady and harmonious.

5. On body movements

The boxing is superior for its speed and swiftness. In particular, its body turning is quicker than the cross retreating. When turning left-forward, the right foot steps to the front of the left foot, body turning right and the right foot following; when turning right-forward, the left foot steps to the front of the right foot, the body turning left and the right foot following. When the body turning backward, the hind foot stands as an pivot and the front foot backwards in a curve to turn the body to 180 degree or 280 degree. The purpose of the body turning is to dodge the opponent's attack at the beginning of a combat and not to initiate one's own attack until the opponent shows his weak points. This is just the superior of Shaolin Mantis Spreading Wings Boxing.

6. On distance, time and reaction

Keep a distance from the opponent, do not initiate attack before he does, but always react faster than him.

Once attacking, do it as quick and accurate as rooster picking grain, with eyes, feet, body and hands functioning simultaneously.

After all, Shaolin Mantis Spreading Wings Boxing has more features of attack and defense. However, to have a good mastery of these principles and skills, one needs a long time of hard work plus comprehension.

Chapter Two The illustration of basic movements of Shaolin Mantis Spreading Wings Boxing

Section 1   Hand forms

1. Various hand forms

（A）Mantis Hook hand

It is the original hand form of Mantis boxing in which the thumb, the index and the middle finger get slightly together while the ring and little finger folded and the wrist bent(Figure 2—1).

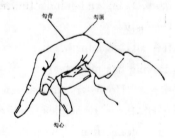

图 2—1

（B）Spreading Wings palm

The four fingers stretch naturally and backward to the back of the hand. The thumb bends and gets against the inner palm edge. The wrist sinks to enforce the outer edge of the little finger and the palm(Figure 2—2).

（C）Willow leaf palm

The index, the middle, the ring and the little fingers get abreast and backward to the back of the hand. The thumb bends against the inner edge of the palm (Figure 2—3).

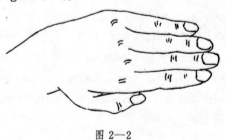

图 2—2

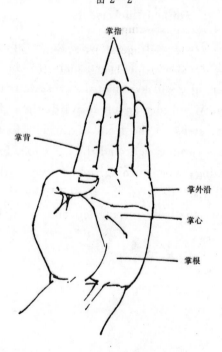

图 2—3

（D）Ba Zi palm

the four fingers get abreast and straight stretched while the thumb posts vertically to the palm edge like a Chinese character Ba (eight)(Figure 2—4).

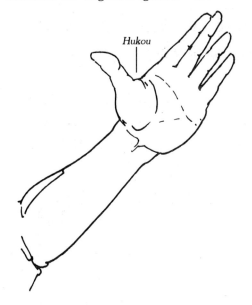

图 2—4

(E) Taiji Boxing palm

The four fingers part and bend slightly, the palm being slightly hollowed; and the thumb forms an arc with the index finger(Figure 2—5).

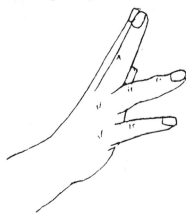

图 2—5

(F) Bagua Zhang hand form

the five fingers part naturally, with the thumb stretching outward and the index finger straight, and the other three fingers fold a little to make the palm

slightly hollowed (Figure 2—6).

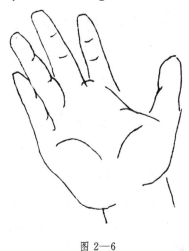

图 2—6

(G) Spiral fist

The five fingers fold inward to form the fist, with the thumb pressed on the second joint of the index, wrist straight, fist clenched and the surface of the fist spiraled from the index to the little finger (Figure 2—7).

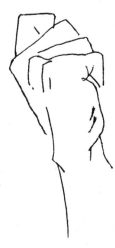

图 2—7

(H) Dingzi fist

The four fingers clench to form the fist, with the second joint of the middle finger protruding, the thumb pressed on the nail of the middle finger, the index,

23

the ring and the little finger squeezed to the point of the middle finger, and the attacking point concentrated on the protruding joint of the middle finger (Figure 2—8).

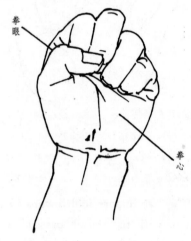

图 2—8

(I) Tile Edge fist

The four fingers fold inward, with the middle joint of each finger protruding as a tile edge, the thumb pressed on the hollow of the index. The hand form looks like a tile and the attacking point is on the tile edge (figure 2—9).

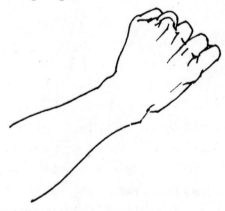

图 2—9

(J) Duckbill fist

The middle, the ring and the little

fingers folded tightly, with the middle joint of the index finger protruding, the thumb pressed on the nail of the index finger and the attacking point located on the protruding part of the index (Figure 2—10).

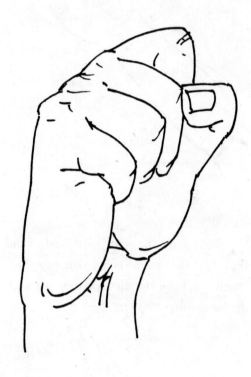

图 2—10

(K) Rubbing fist

The index, the middle and the ring folded inward, the thumb pressed on the hollow of the index, the middle joint of the little finger protruding like a toothbrush as the attacking point. This hand form is often used to rub the opponents eyeballs and the acu-points of the face (Figure 2—11).

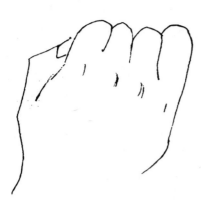

图 2—11

2. The usage of the various hand forms in performance and combat.

" Mantis Hook hand", "Spreading Wings palm", "Willow Leaf palm," "Taiji Boxing palm," and "Bagua Zhang hand form" mentioned above are typical hand forms of the four major boxing schools of Mantis, Shaolin, Taiji and Bagua respectively. In performance of Shaolin Mantis Spreading Wings Boxing, one hand form may be adopted for each school style as "Mantis Hook hand" or "Spreading Wings palm" for Mantis style, "Willow Leaf palm" for Shoalin style, "Taiji Boxing palm" for Taiji style and "Bagua Zhang hand form" for Bagua Zhang style.

Besides, "Spiral fist, Dingzi fist", "Tile Edge fist", "Duckbill fist" and "Rubbing fist" each has its own features while their common distinction is the prominence of the middle joint of one finger. This is aiming at pounding the acupoints of the opponent. The usage of this pounding must be coordinated with body work and movements to make use of the opponent's opening of his acu-points so as to beat him. For example, when pounding the opponent's Qimen point. You must use fake movements to lead the opponent to lift his arms and rise up his inner Qi so that you are able to attack him. When pounding the Huagai point, you must get approaching him with skills and push his head, face or breast so as to force him lift his head and breast and thereby you can pound him on the point with Dingzi fist. "Rubbing fist" is a special hand form used to rub the opponents eyeballs or the acu-points on the face. Its quite effective with its flashing, spinning and rubbing attack.

In a word, when attacking the opponent on acu-points and weak parts, respective movements and tricks must be used to force him to sway before you beat him.

Section 2   Stance

1. Kylin stance

The two feet apart vertically about the width of the shoulder, the front knee bending to half squatting and not beyond the toe, both the front knee and tip toe posting slightly inward while the back foot heel lifted above the ground, and the back tip toe making a 45 degree angle with the front tip toe. Catch the ground with toes, preserve the crotch and keep the head upright. Keep the tiptoe, the nose and the mid-breast on one straight line (Figure 2—12).

图 2—12

2. Side horse stance

Stand in horse stance first and then move front foot tiptoe outward, turning the upper body accordingly. Locate 60% of the body weight on the hind leg while the 40% on the leg that moving outward. When right tiptoe moving outward it's called right side horse stance and, when left tiptoe moving outward, left side horse stance (Figure 2—13).

3. Dingzi stance

Post the feet side by side and bend the knees partly squatting, left sole touching the ground fully while the right heel lifting above with the front sole on the ground. The center of gravity is located on the left foot. It is called Right Dingzi Stance and, when front sole of the left foot touching the ground, Left Dingzi Stance(Figure 2—14).

4. Empty stance

Stand with the feet apart vertically,

hind foot turning outward and the knee bent half squatting, front heel lifting above the ground and instep slightly straining. Keep front sole touching the ground and slightly turning inward, leaving the center of gravity on the hind foot and keeping the upper body upright. When left foot stands front, it is called Left Empty Stance and, when right foot front, Right Empty Stance (Figure 2—15).

图 2—13

5. Twisting stance

Stand with two legs twisting apart, the front foot tiptoe pointing outwards to 45 degree and front sole touching the ground fully, the front leg bending to half squatting and the thigh at horizontal level. Move the hind leg stretching backward with the front sole touching the

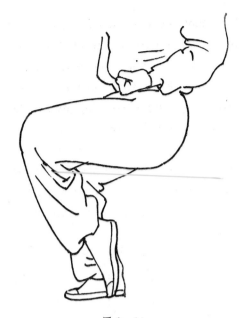

图 2—14

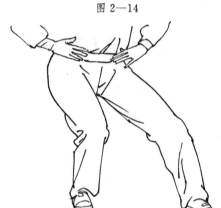

图 2—15

ground and the tiptoe forward (Figure 2—16).

Section 3 Hand work

1. Palm work

(A) Cleaving

Striking downward with the force up to the outer edge of the palm.

(B) Spreading

With the wrist joint as pivot, spread the palm by twisting the wrist up forward.

(C) Stroking

Palm center slanting downward, stroke with palm curving from in front of the forehead to the shoulder blade.

(D) *Zhan*

With the palm hollow slanting upward, strike the chest side of the opponent with the palm edge.

(E) *Tan*

Turn the palm up forward by shaking the wrist with the force concentrated on the back of the hand.

(F) Sticking

Get the four fingers abreast to stick into the opponent on his chest side with the force concentrated on the fingertips.

(G) Cutting

Hand center facing downward, cut horizontally with the palm striking forward.

(H) *Liao*

Strike forward with Mantis hand upward and force concentrated on the back of the hand.

(I) Pressing

Hand center facing downward, press and push down with force concentrated on the palm center.

(J) *Tiao*

Strike up forward, four fingers keeping abreast, thumb folded and wrist setting vertical, with force on the forearm and four fingers.

(K) *Tuo*

Hand center facing upward, push

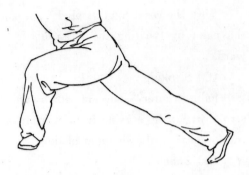

图 2—16

upward with arm bent and force concentrated on the part between the thumb and the index finger.

(L) Pushing

Push with vertical palm from front of the breast, with force reaching the bottom of the palm.

(M) Coiling

Hand center facing inward and the outward, hold the opponent's wrist or forearm by coiling and curving, with the force reaching the wrist and fingers. This palm skill includes six usage as up and down, inward and outward, to and forth.

(N) Ge

Block the attack by turning arm across the front of the face. It has, in addition, four usage as up and down, inward and outward.

2. Fist skills

(A) *Dian*

Forward the arm and shake the wrist to hit the opponent with "Dingzi fist."

(B) *Zhi*

Pound the opponent by clenching fist and stretching arm straight.

(C) Hook

Fist clenched, strike from lower po-

sition up forward with the elbow at 90 degree.

(D) Swing

Fist clenched, strike from the side with the arm bent slightly.

(E) *Cha*

Fist clenched and upper arm lifted, turn forearm inward and stick the opponent forwards or aside.

(F) *Dun*

Fist clenched, strike suddenly downward with the wrist turning inward.

(G) *Quan*

Fist clenched, strike from the side in a circling way.

Section 4   Step work

1. *Yuhuan* step

Right foot steps in half circle in front of the left foot and the left foot steps in half circle to resume the original position. The two feet move in "S" route.

2. *Shanzhan* step

Left (right) foot steps left (right) forward and right (left) foot, front sole sliding on the ground, joins to the left (right) foot accordingly.

3. *Gen* step

The front foot steps forward in half step and the hind foot follows simultaneously with the front sole slipping in half step.

4. *Chuang* step

the front foot slips aside in half step and the hind foot follows simultaneously with the full sole slipping in half step.

5. *Bagua* step

Legs bend slightly and knees touch each other. When stepping forward, keep the sole about one cun (about 0. 24 cm) above the ground and move smoothly with tiptoe forward or a bit outward. Foot drops with full sole firmly.

6. *Hua* step

Stand in cross-leg stance. When one foot slides and moves, the other slides to follow and resume to the original stance.

Section 5   Leg work

1. *Hook*

The left (right) foot steps horizontally and the right (left) foot moves and strikes forward in half circle with the tiptoe up. The front foot stands about 30% of the body weight while the hind foot does the rest.

2. *Tan*

The left (right) foot bears the body weight, while the right (left) leg lifts by bending the knee and makes a sudden kick with tiptoe, instep straining to concentrate the force on the tiptoe.

3. *Bian*

The left leg bends slightly and stands the body weight when the right knee bends to raise the right foot. Straighten the left leg and turn the body left on the pivot of the left front sole when the right foot kicks up forward to attack with the force of the instep and the lower foreleg.

4. *Deng*

The left (right) foot stands the body weight when the right (left) foot kicks forward with the tiptoe hooking back, to attack with the heel.

5. *Bie*

The left (right) foot makes a forward step when the right (left) foot moves forward along the inner side of the left (right) foot and then sweeps back to attack. When attacking, the leg bends slightly before it makes the backward sweeping.

Chapter Three   The illustration of Shaolin Mantis Spreading Wings Boxing series

Section 1   List of the movements

Segment one

1. Commencing form
2. *Diaoshou* and spreading left wing
3. *Diaoshou* and spreading right wing
4. Right block and punch
5. Left block and punch
6. Left waist-cutting
7. White tiger washing face
8. Block, *dian* and kick
9. Closing hands with *Yuhuan* step

Segment two

10. Body turning, *Diaoshou* and cutting
11. Body turning and right wing spreading
12. Thrusting and pressing
13. Double upper-cutting and pressing
14. *Lizhang dunquan*
15. Crotch upper-cutting and *yuanyang* kicking
16. Double closing hands with *Yuhuan* step

Segment three

17. Right elbow receiving
18. Left elbow receiving
19. Right *star picking* with *Bagua* step
20. Left *star picking* with *Bagua* step
21. Gold rooster nodding
22. Palm turning and crotch upper-cutting

23. Over-hand hitting and *yuanyang* kicking
24. Double closing hands with *Yuhuan* step

Segment four

25. Upper pushing and left kicking
26. Upper pushing and right kicking
27. Downward gripping and *quan*-fist hitting
28. Stepping forward and punching
29. Left stroking and right cutting
30. Body turning and right waist-cutting
31. Closing form

Section 2
Illustration of the series

Segment one

1. Commencing form

A) Stand upright with feet shoulder-width apart in parallel, toes pointing forward, arms hanging naturally at sides. Look straight ahead (Fig 2-17).

B) Turn arms outward from two sides up to the front of the forehead, palm centers facing each other and fingers pointing upwards (Fig 2—18).

C) Press the palms down to the front of the abdomen with palm centers facing downward and fingers pointing to each

图 2—17

图 2—18

other. Look straight ahead.

Points to remember: Do not protrude

chest. Hold head and neck erect and shoulders and elbows sunk. Feet are on the ground with full sole. Toes clench to the ground. Knees bend slightly. Anus pulls in and abdomen relaxes. Inhale when hands upward and exhale when hands downward. Keep *qi* in Dantian and be smooth and natural.

2. *Diaoshou* and spreading left wing

A) Right foot moves one step left forward, with right palm center facing outward, wrist twists right outward to make right Mantis Hook hand while the left palm presses rightward, palm facing downward (Fig 2—19).

图 2—19

B) Left foot steps to the front of the right foot. Simultaneously, body turns left and left palm tosses outward with the palm facing downward at the nose level. Right hand follows to the left armpit (Fig 2—20).

Points to remember: Foot stepping,

31

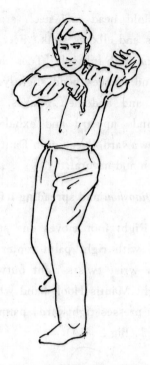

图 2—20

图 2—21

图 2—22

wrist twisting and body turning form a coherent whole. Shoulders and elbows sink. Crotch preserves and waist initiates strength. Inhale when twisting and exhale when tossing outward. Eyesight follow the movements of the hands and notion goes prior to strength.

3. *Diaoshou* **and spreading right wing**

A) Left foot moves one step right forward. Simultaneously, with left palm facing outward, wrist twists left outward to make Mantis Hook hand while right palm presses leftward, hollow facing downward (Fig 2—21).

B) Right foot steps to the front of the left foot, body turns right and right palm tosses outward with the hollow facing downward at the level of the nose. Left hand follows to the right armpit (Fig 2—22).

Points to remember: Foot stepping, wrist twisting and body turning form a coherent whole. Shoulders and elbows sink. Crotch preserves and waist initiates

32

strength. Inhale when twisting and exhale when tossing outward. Eyesight follow the movements of hands and notion goes prior to strength.

4. Right block and punch

A) Right foot steps left forward. Simultaneously, body turns slightly right and right hand swings downward and then upward in a curve to make a pressing by bending the elbow. Left foot steps to make a "side horse-riding" stance by half squatting, while left hand , following the right hand, rises up from under the right armpit in a curve and presses in front of the right hand by bending the elbow. Look ahead (Fig 2—23, 2—24).

图 2—24

图 2—23

B) Body turns left and right fist punches at shoulder level with knuckles inward. Left fist moves to the right side of the chest, with knuckles outward. Eyesight is at the right fist (Fig 2—25).

图 2—25

33

Points to remember: Foot stepping, body turning, hand swinging and twisting form a coherent and harmonious whole. Hand swinging and raising go in curves.

5. Left block and punch

A) Left foot steps left forward. Simultaneously, body turns slightly left, and left hand swings downward and then upward in a curve to make a pressing by bending the elbow. Right foot steps to make a "side horse-riding stance" by half squatting, while right hand, along with the left hand, raises up from under the left armpit in a curve and presses in front of the left hand by bending the elbow. Look ahead (Fig 2—26, 2—27).

图 2—26

B) Body turns right and left fist punches at shoulder level with knuckles

inward. Right fist moves to the left side of the chest, with knuckles outward. Eyesight is at the left fist (Fig 2—28).

图 2—27

Points to remember: Foot stepping, body turning, hand swinging and twisting form a coherent and harmonious whole. Hand swinging and raising go in curves.

6. Left waist-cutting

A) Left foot moves one step forward. Right fist changes to Ba Zi Zhang with palm facing outward and tosses up along the exterior side of the left arm. At the same time, left fist changes to palm and turns inward to the left side of the waist, palm facing upwards. Eyesight is on the right hand (Fig 2—29).

B) Body weight retreats to rest on the left leg. Right foot with tiptoe hook-

图 2—28

图 2—29

by the strength of waist twisting, at the level of the shoulder and with the palm slanting upwards. Right hand pulls back to under the right cheek to make a Mantis Twisting hand. Eyesight is on the left palm (Fig 2—30).

图 2—30

Points to remember: Stepping, tossing, pulling, retreating and sticking form a coherent whole. The sweeping of the right foot is in a curve with the interior side of the heel touching the ground.

7. White tiger washing face

A) Right foot slips right forward and, simultaneously, right hand changes to palm and pushes forward with the palm facing outward at shoulder level. Left palm pulls back to the front of breast, facing right. Eyesight is at the right palm (Fig 2—31).

ing backward sweeps right forward. Simultaneously, left palm fingers sticks out

图 2—31

图 2—32

kick at crotch level. Look at right hand (Fig 2—33).

B) Left foot moves half step to make a Kylin stance and left palm pushes straight forward, while right palm pulls back to under the left armpit with palm facing left. Look at left palm (Fig 2—32).

Points to remember: Coordinate stepping, slanting and pushing to hit with the bottom of the palm.

8. Block, *Dian* and kick

Right foot retreats slightly to half squat, body weight resting on left foot. Left palm pulls back, patting the right elbow, to the front of the left cheek and changes into hook hand. Meanwhile, right thumb presses the middle joint of the index finger to make a *duckbill Dian*.

Body weight rests on the left leg while the right leg raises to make a *Tan*

图 2—33

Points to remember: Left hand defending, right hand attacking and right leg raising act simultaneously. Twist the waist to rest body weight on left foot.

9. Closing hands with *Yuhuan* step

A) Right foot drops over beyond the left foot. Hands changes to palms facing downward and pull in a curve to front of the left breast, with left palm above the right palm, facing inward and downward. Look at the palms (Fig 2—34).

图 2—34

B) Left foot retreats to make a right empty step. Body turns right and, by which, palms push forward and facing forward. Look ahead (Fig 2—35).

Points to remember: Palms and feet work coordinately; pulling goes in curve; and stepping works in "S" route.

Segment two

10. Body turning, *Diaoshou* and rib-cutting

A) Right foot retreats by one step and, with the front part of the left foot as pivot, body turns 180 degree. Right palm pulls by the right side of the body to the front of the right cheek and twists into hook hand, while left palm retreats with left elbow and forearm against the waist (Fig 2—36).

图 2—35

B) Left foot steps forward to make a "side horse-riding" stance, and left palm turns over downward to cut left at shoulder level. Look at left palm (Fig 2—37).

Points to remember: When retreating and body turning, center gravity of the body descends to keep balance. Cut-

37

图 2—36

图 2—37

ting is done with the help of the strength
of the waist and crotch.

38

11. Body turning and right wing spreading

A) Transfer body weight to left leg
and raise right knee to make a single-leg
stand (right foot not beyond the left
knee). Meanwhile, lap the forearms before the breast with right hand on left
hand, palm facing up (Fig 2—38).

图 2—38

B) Retreat right leg by one step.
With the front sole of the left foot as pivot, turn the body right by 270 degree.
Left foot follows to make a Kylin stance.
At the some time, right palm tosses out
along with the body turning, palm facing
downward at eyebrow level. Left palm,
facing downward, presses to right
armpit. Look at right palm (Fig 2—39).

Points to remember: Keep body
gravity steady. Make use of the strength

图 2—39

of the waist and crotch to turn the body and toss the palm.

12. Thrusting and pressing

A) Move left foot one step forward. Turn right palm inwardly with palm facing up. Twist wrist left with force inwardly. Toss the left palm from right armpit along the exterior side of the right arm. Pull the right arm back spinning inwardly with the bottom of the thumb touching the right side of the chest and palm facing forward and a little downward.

B) Toss the left hand forward and pull it back by the front of the face and make a twisting hand form at the left cheek side. Stand on the left foot and make a forward-backward sweeping with the right leg, to make a left bow-stance. Simultaneously, toss and press the right hand forward in Ba Zi Zhang, palm facing ahead and *Hukou* up, at shoulder level. Look at right palm (Fig 2—40, 2—41, 2—42).

图 2—40

图 2—41

Points to remember: Keep the sweeping leg strained with the force initiated from the heel. When pressing, initiate the force from the bottom of the palm to the fingers.

39

図 2—42

図 2—43

13. Double upper cutting and pressing

A) Change hands to palms with right palm moving by the front of shoulder and breast to the crotch then thrusting up by the interior side of the right thigh, facing leftward at the eyebrow level. At the same time, left palm sticks down to the

40

crotch, facing rightwards (Fig 2—43).

B) Left palm moves by the right armpit and elbow in a circle and sets upright in front of the breast, facing outwards; right palm turns back by the interior side of left forearm to the front of the belly, facing leftward. Look ahead.

(C) Move the right foot ahead and push forward with two palms from the breast. Left palm posts above the right palm, both facing outwards. Look at the palms (Fig 2—44, 2—45).

図 2—44

Points to remember: When pushing and pressing, the two palms joint strength inwardly. The palms push while the fingers press, both of which make use of the strength from the waist and crotch. The dual thrusting and pressing act in continuity.

14. *Lizhang Dunquan*

A) Set left palm in front of the breast, palm facing rightwards. Pull right palm back and turn it over into fist

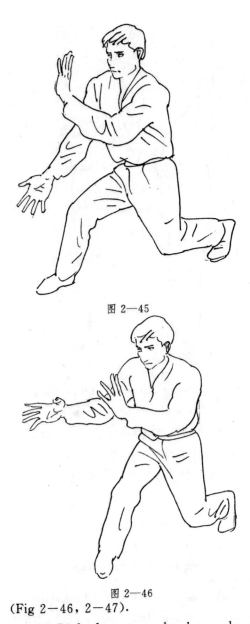

图 2—45

15. Crotch upper-cutting and *yuanyang* kicking

A) Right fist turns into palm and tosses towards the front of the right knee with the elbow as pivot and palm facing right. Body gravity sinks and transfers to right leg. Left palm sets in front of the right shoulder. Look at right hand (Fig 2—49).

图 2—47

图 2—46

(Fig 2—46, 2—47).

B) Right foot steps ahead to make a Kylin stance. Right fist punches straight forward with knuckles upwards, at the shoulder level. Left palm sets upright next to the interior side of the right forearm. Look at right fist (Fig 2—48).

Points to remember: Two hands work simultaneously and so do the right foot stepping and right hand punching.

B) Right palm tosses up to attack with the back of the palm, hollowing inward at the brow level. Left palm sets under the right elbow, facing outward. Simultaneously, body rises and weight rests on left leg. Raise right knee to make a whip-attack with the right instep towards the direction that the right palm faces (Fig 2—50).

Points to remember: Body presses

图 2—48

图 2—49

图 2—50

forward when hand tosses. Knees preserve inward. Strength reaches to four fingers and, when tossing with hollowed palm, to the back of the palm.

16. Double closing hands with *Yuhuan* step

A) Right foot drops back, before the left knee, to beyond the left foot. Hands change into palm with hollows downward and fingers leftward, turning along with the body, then lift in front of the breast. Left palm get above the right palm, hollows facing in and downward (Fig 2—51, 2—52, 2—53).

B) Left foot retreats to sevenstarstance. Body turns right. Palms push forward along with the body turning,

42

hollows facing forward and *Hukou* upwards. Look ahead (Fig 2—54).

Points to remember: Palm work and step work coordinate in harmony. Palm turning goes in curve. Feet move in "S" stepping.

Segment three

17. Right elbow receiving

A) Body weight moves backward and rests on left leg, body turning left. Right foot crosses to the front of the left foot two feet apart, front sole touching the ground to make an empty stance. Left forearm lifts by bending the elbow which points forward. Left palm sets before the right shoulder with the hollow facing outward. Right palm stretches forward from under the left armpit, facing up at the left elbow level (Fig 2—55).

图 2—51

图 2—53

图 2—52

图 2—54

图 2—55

图 2—56

B) Right foot retreats one step back, body turning right. Two palms change to hook hands and pull back with the body turning, right hand to the front of the right shoulder with index finger points forward and slightly downward, and left hand to the right side of the chest with the index pointing up. Left foot backs half a step to make a left Ding Zi stance (Fig 2—56).

Points to remember: Hand pulling and foot backing move simultaneously. Strength generates from waist. Keep backbone erect and do not protrude chest.

18. Left elbow receiving

A) left foot retreats one step to the left. Right forearm lifts by bending the elbow which points forward. Right palm sets in front of the left shoulder, palm hollow facing out. Left palm stretches forward from under the right armpit, palm hollow facing up at the right elbow level (Fig 2—57).

B) Left foot retreats one step back, body turning left. Two palms change to hook hands and pull back along with the body turning, left hand to the front of the right shoulder with index finger pointing forward and slightly downward, and right hand to the left side of the chest with index pointing upward. Right foot backs half a step to make a right Ding Zi stance (Fig 2—58).

Points to remember: Hand pulling and foot backing move simultaneously. Strength generates from the waist. Keep backbone erect and do not protrude chest.

44

图 2—57

图 2—58

19. Right *star picking* with *Bagua* step

A) Right foot crosses right-forward and left foot turns right with the body. Legs cross to each other. Simultaneously, right hand changes to Bagua Zhang with hollow upward and spires out from under the left armpit to above the right tiptoe vertically at the eyebrow level, with palm facing inward. Left hand changes to palm and sets under the right elbow, facing outward. Look at right palm (Fig 2—59).

图 2—59

B) Body continues to turn right. Left foot steps around the right foot with tiptoe pointing inward. Two hands keep the same palm form while right palm leads up to make a pivoting Bagua Zhang. Wade four steps to finish a circle (Fig 2—60).

45

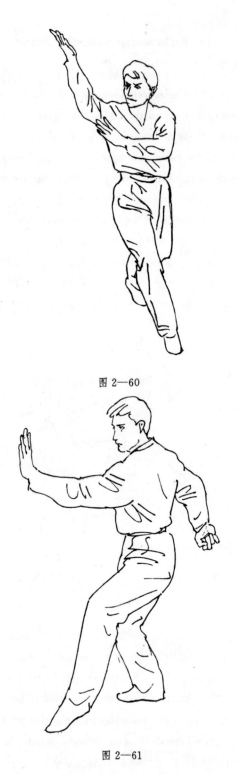

图 2—60

图 2—61

ly, right palm changes into fist and pulls downward and backward to the hind of the body. Left palm thrusts upward with the hollow rightward at the eyebrow level. Look at left palm (Fig 2—61).

points to remember: This movement is similar to that of Bagua Zhang. When thrusting, the left thumb is against the palm and, when pulling backward, the right palm should not be beyond the waist.

20. Left *star-picking* with *Bagua* step

A) Body turns right and weight rests on right leg. Left heel lifts and retreats to the interior side of the right foot to make a "Ding Zi" stance with the left front sole touching the ground. Along with the body tuning, left palm holds to the front of the abdomen, hollow facing up and *Hukou* ahead. Right fist changes into palm and lifts to the front of the breast, *Hukou* facing inward and hollow downward to face the left palm. Look at right palm (Fig 2—62).

B) Body turns left. Left foot moves in curve with tiptoe and drops in the left front. Left palm turns out from the right armpit while right palm sets under the left elbow. These are the same with the movements of "right star-picking with Bagua step", but the opposite direction (Fig 2—63). Then, pull the left leg to make right empty stance. Pull with left hand and thrust with right palm. Look at right palm (Fig 2—64).

Points to remember: The same with

C) Right foot retreats one step to make a left *empty* stance. Simultaneous-

46

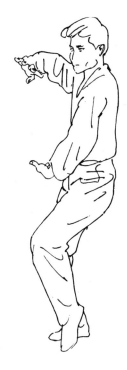

图 2—62

图 2—63

"right star-picking with Bagua step".

21. Gold rooster nodding

A) Body twists and turns right. Left leg moves one step forward. At the same time, right palm changes into fist and pulls back to the front of right side of chest, knuckles forward. Left fist changes into palm and lifts to the front chest and presses inward until 15 cm to the chest, palm facing right and downward (Fig 2—65).

图 2—64

B) Left foot moves further about half a step and body turns left. Meantime, right fist punches straight out and left fist retreats to the right armpit (Fig 2—66). Left fist punches straight out and right fist backs to left armpit. Look at left fist (Fig 2—67).

C) Left foot moves another half a step and right foot follows behind. Mean-

47

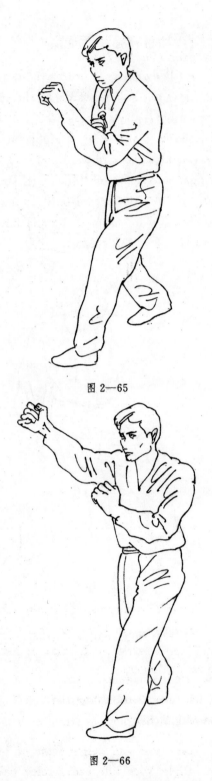

图 2—65

图 2—66

D) Weight gravity rests on left leg. Right leg lifts and kicks forward with the heel at the crotch level. Meantime, right fist makes a up-hook attack. Knuckles outward at the nose level, and left fist changes into palm and sets at the interior side of the right forearm. Look at right fist (Fig 2—70).

图 2—67

Points to remember: Attacking of straight blow, swing and hook forms a coherent whole without pause. Hand work and step work done in coordination.

22. Palm turning and crotch upper-cutting

Right foot drops in the front to make a low horse-riding stance. Body twists right and, meantime, right fist changes into palm and tosses with elbow as pivot

time, make a right swing (fig 2—68) and then a left swing attack (Fig 2—69).

48

图 2—68

图 2—69

along with the direction of the dropping foot, palm facing out and *Hukou* down. Left palm sets at the interior side of the

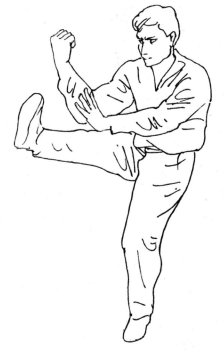

right shoulder as protection. Look at right palm (Fig 2—71).

图 2—70

图 2—71

Points to remember: The palm tossing strength starts from the waist and crotch and reaches to the tips of index and middle fingers.

23. Over-hand hitting and *Yuanyang* kicking

Body rises and weight rests on left foot. Right knee lifts and foreleg pulls back to make a "whip attack" with the instep towards right. Meantime, right

49

palm pulls back and thrusts upward with the back of the hand, palm facing inward at the head level. Left palm sets at the crotch as protection, facing inward. Look at the right palm (Fig 2—72).

(Fig 2—73, 2—74, 2—75).

图 2—73

图 2—72

Points to remember: Right palm thrusting strength concentrates on the back of the hand. Right foot whipping clutches with force. The thrusting and whipping finish simultaneously.

24. Double closing hands with *Yuhuan* step

A) Right foot drops beyond the left foot. Hands change into palms, facing down and fingers left. Two palms stroke downward along with the body turning and lift to the left front of the breast, left palm above right palm, both facing inward and downward. Look at two palms

图 2—74

B) Left foot retreats to right *empty*

图 2—75

图 2—76

stance. Meantime, body turns right and palms push forward, hollows facing

ahead and *Hukou* up. Look ahead (Fig 2 —76).

Points to remember: Palm closing and foot retreating work in harmonious coordination. The closing and stroking should be done in curve and feet moving in "S"route.

Segment four

25. Upper pushing and left kicking

A) Right foot backs one step, body turns 180 degree right and legs cross to each other. Along with the body turning, right palm turns outward to make a *Diaoshou* in front of the forehead, hollow outward. Meantime, left palm pushes upward along a parallel route with the curving of the right palm, fingers apart, hollow up and *Hukou* leftward. Look at left palm (Fig 2—77).

B) Body weight rests on the right foot, while left knee lifts and crotch collects to kick sideward at the waist level. Look left-forward (Fig 2—78).

Points to remember: Lower the gravity when body turning. Keep balance with sunken shoulders and elbows. Keep backbone erect and do not protrude the chest. Eyesight follows hands.

26. Upper pushing and right kicking

A) Left foot drops to the ground with tiptoe pointing outward. Body turns left while right foot clutches inward to cross with the left foot. Along with body turning, left palm turns outward and makes a *Diaoshou* at the left side of the

51

图 2—77

图 2—78

left palm, fingers apart, hollow upward and *Hukou* rightward. Look at right palm (Fig 2—79).

图 2—79

B) Body gravity rests on left foot while right knee lifts and crotch collects to kick sideward at the waist level. Look right-forward (Fig 2—80).

Points to remember: The same with "upper pushing and left kicking".

27. Downward gripping and *quan-fist hitting*

A) Right foot drops and left foot steps ahead. Meantime palms change into fists by gripping. Right fist ahead of the left, knuckles up (Fig 2—81).

B) Right leg sweeps forward and backward to make left "bow" stance. Meantime two hands cross in front of the breast and part downward and turn for-

forehead, hollow outward. Meantime right palm pushes upward along with the

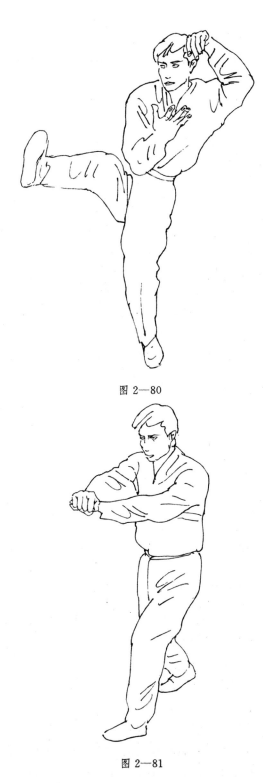

图 2—80

the shoulder level, while left hand sets at the interior side of the right forearm. Look at right fist (Fig 2—82, 2—83).

图 2—82

Points to remember: Stepping, gripping and sweeping form a coherent whole and movements be swift and coordinate.

28. Stepping forward and punching

Right foot steps ahead. Left fist changes into palm and covers along the right arm, hollow facing downward and *Hukou* inward. Meantime right fist pulls back to the waist (Fig 2—84). Right fist punches out of the back of left palm, knuckles outward at the shoulder level. Left palm changes into fist and sets at the interior side of the right shoulder. Look at right fist (Fig 2—85).

Points to remember: Foot stepping and palm covering act simultaneously;

图 2—81

ward in a curve. Right fist makes a forward swing attack with knuckles up at

53

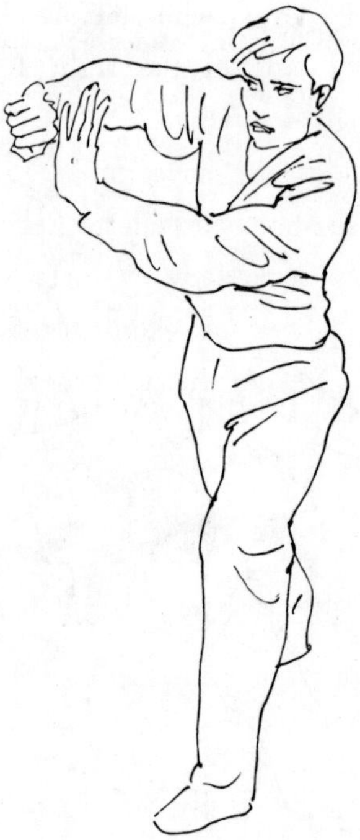

图 2—83

29. Left stroking and right cutting

Right foot slips half step forward and body turns slightly left to half "Horse-riding" stance. Left fist changes into palm, facing down and slightly outward, and strokes out along the exterior side of the right arm. Meantime, right fist backs to waist and changes into palm. Facing up, and then turns to face down and cuts rightwards at the shoulder level. Left palm changes into hook hand and sets at the interior side of the right shoulder, hollow facing right. Look at right palm (Fig 2—86, 2—87).

图 2—85

图 2—84

and foot drops when fist punches. Inhale when covering and exhale when punching.

Points to remember: Cutting be done with the strength from body turning and foot dropping, reaching the exterior edge of the palm.

54

图 2—86

图 2—87

30. Body turning and right waist-cutting

A) Right foot moves one step to the right side and body turns left. Right palm turns outwards and twists in curve past abdomen, left armpit and forehead to make a *Diaoshou* at the right cheek (Fig 2—88).

图 2—88

B) Body twists left. Left hand turns into palm facing out, Hukou downwards, and twists in curve past breast and forehead to make a *Diaoshou* at the left cheek. Meantime, body weight transfers to right leg, body turning right, and left foot hooks with tiptoe pointing upward and big toe clutching inward to hook ahead. Right hand changes into palm facing up and sticks out downward and forward (Fig 2—89).

55

图 2—89

Points to remember: When making *Diaoshou*, hands move in curve. When foot hooking or palm sticking, waist twisting and crotch sinking are necessary.

31. Closing form

A) Left leg lifts and move half a step forward and, meantime, both palms pull back to the front of breast, hollows facing inward and fingers downward. Both arms lift and wrists twist in front of face, to turn palms over, hollows facing up at the eyebrow level. Look at the palms (Fig 2—90).

B) Right foot follows up to parallel the left foot, shoulder-width apart. Meantime both palms drop and part by the sides of body and then hold up to above the front of forehead, hollows fac-

ing each other and fingers pointing up (Fig 2—91). Then press the palms to the front of the abdomen with hollows facing down and palm fingers pointing to each other. Look ahead (Fig 2—92).

Points to remember: Lift the leg and pull the palms simultaneously. When pressing palms, keep backbone erect and do not protrude chest. Concentrate strength on the exterior edges of the palms. Inhale when holding palms upward and exhale when pressing down.

图 2—90

图 2—91

图 2—92

Chapter Four The illustration of movements of Shaolin Mantis Spreading Wings Boxing in combat

Section 1   List of movements

1. Commencing form
2. *Diaoshou* and left wing spreading
3. *Diaoshou* and right wing spreading
4. Right block and push
5. Left block and push
6. Left waist-cutting
7. White tiger washing face
8. Block, *Dian* and kick
9. Closing hands with *Yuhuan* step
10. Body turning, *Diaoshou* and cutting
11. Body turning and right wing spreading
12. Thrusting and pressing
13. Double upper-cutting and pressing
14. *Lizhang Dunquan*
15. Crotch upper-cutting and *Yuanyang* kicking
16. Right elbow receiving
17. Left elbow receiving
18. Right star-picking with Bagua step
19. Left star-picking with Bagua step
20. Gold rooster nodding
21. Upper pushing and left kicking
22. Upper pushing and right kicking
23. Downward gripping and *Quan*-fist hitting
24. Stepping forward and punching
25. Left stroking and right cutting
26. Body turning and right waist-cutting
27. Closing form

Section 2   Illustration of combating movements

This chapter deals with the combating use of the series of Shoalin Mantis Spreading Wings Boxing. For the convenience of illustrating, we simulate the two combatants as A in black, and B in white. The attacks of A are exemplified only with straight-blow.

1. Commencing form

A is left and B right, standing with feet apart. Look at each other (Fig 2—93).

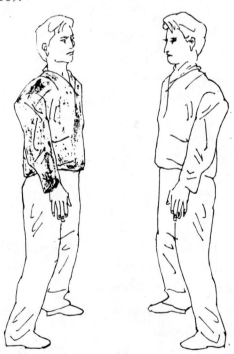

图 2—93

Points to remember: Both A and B

adjust breathing and get up steam to be in best condition.

2. *Diaoshou* and left wing spreading

A is left and B right. A steps forward with right foot and punches B on the chest with right fist. B turns rightward swiftly and moves one step ahead to grab A's wrist (forearm or elbow) by right arm (Fig 2—94), and bends left arm to hit A's arm and steps with left foot ahead at the same time. Consecutively, B turns body left forcefully and attacks A on the neck and cheek with left palm (Fig 2—95).

图 2—94

Points to remember: When grabbing, be accurate and quick with force in the fingers. The left hand hitting must be heavy and attacking fast with the force by waist twisting.

3. *Diaoshou* and right wing spreading

A is right and B left. A steps forward with left foot and punches B on the chest with left hand. B turns leftward swiftly and moves left foot one step ahead to grab A's wrist (forearm or elbow) with left wrist (Fig 2-96), and bends right arm to hit A's arm and steps right foot ahead at the same time. Consecutively, B turns body right forcefully and attacks A on the neck and cheek with right palm (Fig 2—97).

Points to remember: The same with "Diaoshou and left wing spreading".

4. Right block and punch

A is right and B left. A steps forward with right foot and punches B with right straight blow on the chest. B bends right arm to keep it off and grabs A's wrist (forearm or elbow) at the same time and steps ahead with right foot to A's right side. Consecutively, B moves left foot one step ahead and clutches inward to block A's right heel, left knee propping against A's exterior side of foreleg, and bends left arm to press A's right arm with wrist clutching A's shoulder pit and left elbow punching A's right chest (Fig 2—98). If A retreats, B changes right palm into fist and jabs A's right temple (Fig 2—99).

Points to remember: B must grab on time. Left foot stepping and left elbow punching work simultaneously, with combined force of waist and arm. Left foot clutches A's right heel and makes him unable to change position. Right hand jabbing must be as fast as light.

5. Left block and punch

A is left and B right. A steps ahead

59

图 2—95

right arm to press A's left arm while clutching A's shoulder pit with wrist and punching A's left chest with elbow (Fig 2 —100). If A retreats, B changes left palm into fist and jabs A on the temple (Fig 2—101).

图 2—97

图 2—96

图 2—98

with left foot and jabs B with left hand in the chest. B swiftly bends left arm to keep it off and grabs A's wrist (forearm or elbow) at the same time, moves left foot to the left side of A and moves right foot one step forward to clutch A's left heel while blocking A's exterior side of A's foreleg with right knee, and bends

Points to remember: The same with "right block and punch", but opposite

图 2—99

palm, and then grabs A's elbow joint with right hand (Fig 2—102). A retreats with right foot moving backward while B pulls with right hand, hooks A's left heel with right foot and sticks into A's right chest with left palm (Fig 2—103).

图 2—101

图 2—100

movement directions.

6. Left waist-cutting

A is right and B left. A steps with right foot forward and jabs B on the face with right hand. B swiftly bats A's exterior side of his right forearm with left

图 2—102

Points to remember: B must bats A's right forearm in time in order to change A's attacking direction. Hooking

61

图 2—103

the strength be initiated from body turning and waist twisting and backward stretching of the left leg. The upper body and lower body must coordinate and body work and step work must be flexible. The crossing pushing of the two palms be fast and coherent.

图 2—104

A's left heel is to prevent him from retreating. Palm sticking should be done forcefully with the strength of waist twisting and crotch turning.

7. White tiger washing face

A is right and B left. A steps ahead with right foot and attacks B in the chest with right straight blow. B swiftly lowers upper body and pushes A left forward with right palm on the interior side of A's right forearm and, meantime, steps up with right foot left forward (Fig 2—104). A retreats to dodge and B turns right forward to push A on the face with left palm (Fig 2—105).

Points to remember: To push with right palm, B should turn upper body slightly right to dodge A's attacking direction. When pushing with left palm,

图 2—105

8. Block, *Dian* and kick

A is right and B left. A steps up with right foot ahead and attacks B in the chest with right hand straight blow. B moves half step forward with left foot, slaps rightward on A's exterior side of right elbow, clutches its interior side with wrist locking and pulls it downward and then left upward-backward. A retreats. B kicks A on the knee (or crotch) and jabs A on *Huagai* point in the chest with right duckbill fist. (Fig 2—106)

Points to remember: Slapping, kicking and jabbing work in coherent whole. Clutching must be done with the strength of the wrist, and jabbing and kicking simultaneously.

9. Closing hands with *Yuhuan* step

A is right and B left. A steps up with left foot ahead and kicks B in the crotch. B swiftly move right leg to cross back-leftward to protect the crotch and, meantime, cuts A's ankle with left palm and cuts his knee joint (or shin bone) with right palm (Fig 2—107, 2—108). Consecutively, B backs half step with left foot, gets palms in front of chest and then pushes forward in A's chest, right foot advancing half step (Fig 2—109).

Points to remember: Be flexible with crossing *Yuhuan* step. Pay attention to protecting the crotch. Concentrate strength on the exterior side of palms when cutting. Use the strength from waist twisting when pushing with both arms.

10. Body turning, *Diaoshou* and cutting

A is hind and B front. A steps up with right foot ahead and attacks B on the right shoulder with right hand. B swiftly turns body right backward, right foot retreating half step, and grasps A's right arm (or collar) and pulls it backward (Fig 2—110). Consecutively, B turns body further rightward and steps up with left foot to lock A's front foot heel and, meantime, cuts A in the right chest with left palm (Fig 2—111).

Points to remember: Movements are in coherence and body backing, turning and grasping in coordination. Left palm cutting must be quick and forceful.

11. Body turning and right wing spreading

A is right and B left. A steps up with right foot ahead and attacks B on the head with right straight blow from aside or behind. B swiftly turns rightward and steps up with left foot and, meantime, bends right arm to parry A's forearm (Fig 2—112). Consecutively, B strokes and pulls A's right elbow and forearm outward and downward, then, continues to turn rightward and steps up to hit A on the head or hack with right elbow. Next, B turns 360 degree from behind A to A's left side and slaps A on the left ear or throat with right palm. (Fig 2—113, 2—114)

图 2—106

图 2—108

图 2—107

图 2—109

图 2—110

图 2—112

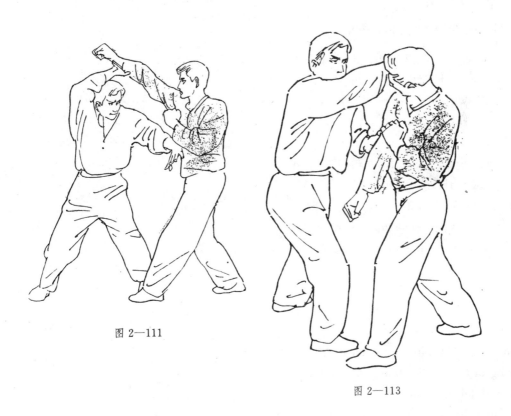

图 2—111

图 2—113

图 2—114

Points to remember: B parries in time and steps up, strokes, pulls and hits fast with coherence of waist turning and vigorous slapping.

12. Thrusting and pressing

A is right and B left. A steps up with left foot ahead and punches B in the chest. B swiftly twists right palm outward to grasp A's right wrist (or forearm) and moves right foot one step forward (Fig 2—115). No sooner than A pulls back with right hand, B grabs A's right elbow and pulls it with left hand and, successively, steps up to behind A's right leg with right foot to block it and lifts it over backward with trip and, meantime, jabs A's throat with thumb and right index finger (Fig 2—116).

Points to remember: To grasp A's wrist with right hand is to defeat A's attacking direction. Grabbing A's right elbow with left hand must be in time. Stepping up, lifting leg over and jabbing

66

throat should go in coherence. The jabbing must be forceful with palm heel pressing down.

13. Double upper-cutting and pressing

A is right and B left. A steps up with left foot ahead and attacks B on the face with left straight blow. B swiftly steps up with right foot and parries outward with right forearm (Fig 2—117). A gets back left hand and attacks B in the chest with right straight blow. B steps up with left foot and parries outward with left arm (Fig 2—118). Consecutively, B steps up with right foot entering into the interior side of A's left leg and pushes A on the face and crotch with left palm up and right palm down (Fig 2—119).

图 2—115

图 2—116

图 2—118

图 2—117

图 2—119

Points to remember: The parrying and entering should be done in time. When pushing, fingers should clutch inward to form a combined strength of both forward and downward.

14. *Lizhang Dunquan*

A is left and B right. A steps up with right foot ahead and attacks B in the chest with left straight blow. B swiftly slaps the wrist of the attacking hand downward and clutches fiercely to pull it back and, meantime, tramples on A's left foot with right foot (Fig 2—120). A retreats when B steps ahead with right foot and jabs A in the ribs with right hand in Ding Zi fist (Fig 2—121).

Points to remember: Slap and pull in time. Trample A's left foot to prevent A from retreating. *Dunquan* is used by making used of the strength of A's left arm pulling. Set left palm at the chest for defense.

15. Crotch upper-cutting and *Yuanyang* kicking

A is left and B right. A steps ahead with right foot and attacks B in the chest with right straight blow. B swiftly parries with left palm outward (Fig 2—122) and steps up with right foot towards A's crotch and, meantime, presses body downward to slap A's crotch with right palm (fig 2—123). A retreats to defend with hand down when B rises to slap A on the face with right handback and at the same time kicks A on the waist or left check with right foot (Fig 2—124).

Points to remember: Parry in time and step up fast simultaneously with right palm slapping on A's crotch. Slap with right palm fiercely to hit A's nose, mouth and eyes. Kick fast with force and accuracy.

16. Right elbow receiving

A is left and B right. A steps ahead with left foot and attacks B in the chest with right straight blow. B steps forward to the right side of A with left foot and lifts right hand to grasp A's right elbow and grabs A's right wrist with left hand (Fig 2—125). Consecutively, B retreats half step with right foot and breaks A's right wrist leftward and downward and, meantime, pulls right hand up to scratch A on Shaohai point with the thumb (Fig 2— 126).

Points to remember: Grasp elbow in time and scratch the acu-point with force and accuracy. Retreat and pull in a sudden speed. Break A's wrist fiercely.

17. Left elbow receiving

A is right B left. A steps ahead with left foot and attacks B in the chest with left straight blow. B swiftly steps ahead with right foot to A's left side, and meantime, lifts left hand to grasp A's right elbow and grabs A's left wrist with right hand (fig 2—127). Consecutively, B retreats half step with left foot, breaks A's left wrist rightward and downward and pulls left hand up to scratch A at Shaohai point with thumb (Fig 2—128).

图 2—120

图 2—122

图 2—121

图 2—123

图 2—124

图 2—126

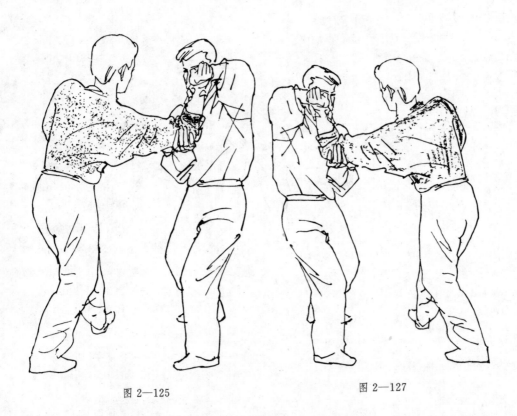

图 2—125

图 2—127

图 2—128

18. Right star-picking with Bagua step

A is left and B right. A steps ahead with left foot and attacks B on the chest with right straight blow. B steps with right foot to A's right side and twists right hand inwardly and stretches it against A's arm with the exterior side of arm (Fig 2—129). Meantime, B pushes A on the right elbow with left palm to make A turn left. Consecutively, B steps forward with left foot, toes pointing inward, withdraws right foot, pushes A's waist with left elbow and clutches and pulls A's throat or jaw with right hand (Fig 2—130).

Points to remember: Step ahead in curve. Make A off balance by pushing his waist with left elbow and pulling his throat or jaw.

19. Left star-picking with Bagua step

A is right and B left. A steps ahead with left foot and attacks B on the chest with left straight blow. B steps with left foot to A's left side and twists left hand inwardly and stretches it to be against A's arm with exterior side of the arm (Fig 2—131). Meantime, B pushes A on the left elbow with right palm to make A turn right. Consecutively, B steps forward with right foot, toes pointing inward, withdraws left foot, pushes A's waist with right elbow and clutches and pulls A's throat or jaw with left hand (Fig 2—132).

Points to remember: Step in curves. Make A off balance by pushing A's waist with right elbow and pulling A with left hand.

20. Gold rooster nodding

A is left and B right. A steps ahead with right foot and attacks B in the chest with right straight blow. B swiftly steps forward with right foot to A's right side and turns right and outward and downward to parry it and, meantime, presses A's right elbow with left palm and steps forward to trample A's front foot and punches A on the face with right straight blow (Fig 2—133). A dodges B's right straight and B gives A a left straight instead (Fig 2—134). A fends off the blow with right arm and attacks B on the face with left straight blow. B shoves the blow aside with left palm and gives A consecutive attacks on both temples with left and right swing attacking (Fig 2—135, 2—136). A retreats and protects two sides with arms when B steps ahead

71

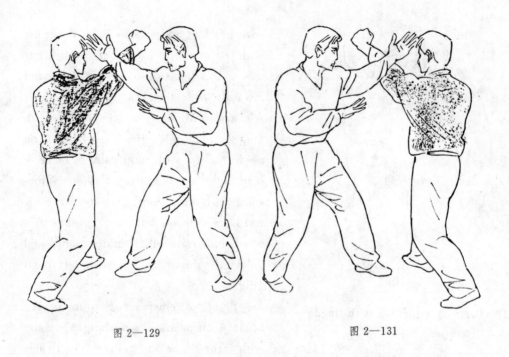

图 2—129   图 2—131

图 2—130   图 2—132

图 2—133

图 2—135

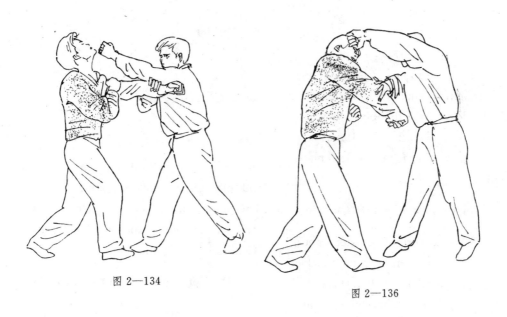

图 2—134

图 2—136

to punch A on the jaw with upper hook and kick A at the crotch or abdomen (Fig 2—137).

ribs (Fig 2—139).

图 2—138

图 2—139

图 2—137

Points to remember: It is a combination of straight, swing and hook attacks, which should be used flexibly. Attacking and defending work simultaneously. Stepping and boxing form a coherent coordination.

21. Upper pushing and left kicking

A is left and B right. A steps ahead with left foot and attacks B on the face with right straight blow. B retreats half step back with right foot, body turning right, and grasps A's right wrists with right hand, pulls and twist it outward (Fig 2—138) and, meantime, pushes A's right elbow with left palm and kicks A with left foot on the crotch, chest, or

Points to remember: Grasp in time and place and twist immediately after. The pulling and pushing compose a lever strength to break the opponents arm. Kicking be quick and heavy.

22. Upper pushing and right kicking

A is left and B right. A steps ahead with right foot and attacks B in the face with left hand. B retreats half step back with left foot, body turning left, grasps A's left wrist with left hand, pulls and twists it outward （Fig 2 — 140） and， meantime， pushes A's left elbow with right palm and kicks A with right foot on the crotch, chest or ribs （Fig 2—141）.

图 2—140

图 2—141

Points to remember: Same with "upper pushing and left kicking".

23. Downward gripping and *quan*-fist hitting

A is right and B left. A steps ahead and attacks B on the face with right straight blow. B swiftly slaps A's right wrist outward with left palm and cuts A's right arm with right palm （Fig 2—142）. Consecutively, B steps ahead with right foot getting behind A's right foot to block it, hits A on the left temple or check with a right swing blow, and lifts A's right leg over with trip by the right leg （Fig 2— 143）.

图 2—142

Points to remember: Left palm slapping, right foot blocking and right palm cutting be done almost at the same time and in coordination. Right palm cutting be vigorous, and lifting and swinging coherent.

24. Stepping forward and punching

B is right and A left. A steps ahead

图 2—143

with right foot and attacks B on the chest. B swiftly steps ahead to trample A's right foot with right foot and slaps A's wrist with left palm. Meantime, B twists body leftward and punches A on the Huagai point of the chest with right straight blow (Fig 2—144).

Points to remember: Stepping ahead to trample A is to prevent his retreating and left palm slapping is to fend A's attack aside. Right straight blow be done with the strength by waist twisting.

25. Left stroking and right cutting

B is right and A left. A steps ahead with left foot and attacks B on the chest with left straight blow. B parries it with left hand (Fig 2—145) and grabs A's left wrist at the same time. Consecutively, B steps forward with right foot, body turn-

ing left, and cuts A in left chest with right palm (Fig 2—146).

Points to remember: B must parry A's attack in time and grab A's wrist immediately. Stepping and cutting must be done quickly and vigorously. And cutting be done with the strength of waist turning.

图 2—144

图 2—145

26. Body turning and right waist-cutting

A is left and B right. A steps ahead with left foot and attacks B on the face

76

图 2—146

with right straight blow. B swiftly steps forward with right foot to A's left side, body turning right, simultaneously, pushes and garbs A's right elbow with right hand and pulls it rightward (Fig 2—147). A withdraws right fist and attacks B on the face with left straight blow. B pushes and grabs A's left elbow with left hand and pulls it leftward, meantime, shuffling in curve with left foot heel, lifts A's right foot over with trip, body turning left, and sticks into A's left ribs with right hand fingers (Fig 2—148).

Points to remember: Stepping to A's left side is to dodge A's attack and pulling with right hand is to force A to release left blow. Lifting over is to prevent A from retreat and is done simultaneously with palm sticking. And sticking should be vigorous with the strength of waist turning and crotch turning.

27. Closing form

A is left and B right. A steps ahead

with right foot and starts to lift hands when B steps forward to press them (Fig 2—149). A tries to retreat when B lifts left foot to kick A in the crotch with toes forward and, meantime, turns palms up to hit A on the face (Fig 2—150, 2—151).

图 2—147

Points to remember: Kick with vigor and accuracy. Turn palms to hit with the handback and hit the opponent's eyeballs with the middle finger nails.

77

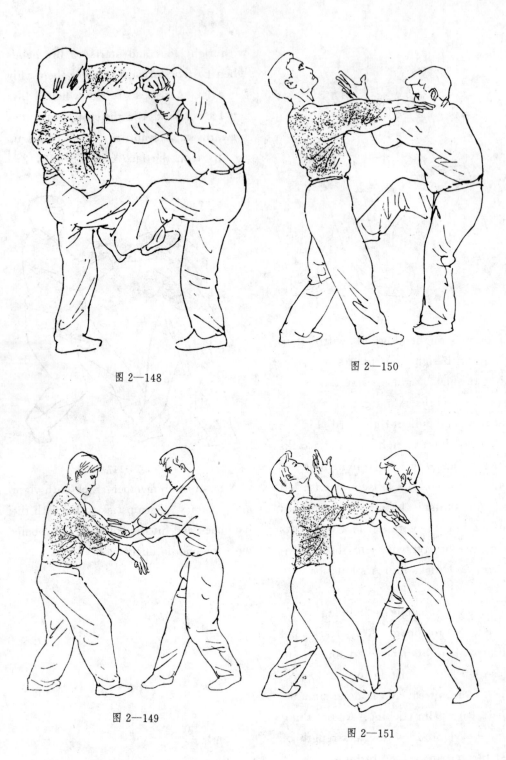

图 2—148

图 2—150

图 2—149

图 2—151

Part Three   Kungfu

Chapter One   Essentials of Kungfu

Section 1   Internal exercises

1. Standing exercises

There are a number of standing exercises. Each has its own way of practice and special system. The following is to introduce the methods and essentials of the three stances (high, middle and low) of standing exercises, taking horse-riding stance as an example.

High stance of standing exercise requires standing with feet shoulder-width apart, knees relaxed and bent slightly and toes pointing straight forward, arms hanging naturally at sides or, palm hollows facing each other like holding a ball or left palm overlapping on the right palm, hollows up, set at the front of the belly (the pubic region). Keep the body upright, eyes and mouth slightly closed, chin drawn slightly inward, tongue resting on the hard palate, abdomen drawn slightly in and concentration at Dantian point (Hypogastrium) (Fig 3—152).

A) Essentials: the three acu-points, Baihui point and two Yongquan points,

form an isosceles triangle in which Baihui point is at the vertex angle and the two Yongquan points at the ends of the bot-

图 3—152

tom line. The body weight rests at the intersect between the vertical line and the bottom line. Toes clutched slightly to the ground, weight evenly distributed on two soles and the whole body relaxed in tranquillity with natural breath.

79

图 3—153

图 3—154

The time of the standing exercise should be decided according to one's particular physique. It's advisable to do it for two hours both in the morning and evening. At the beginning, those who are of stronger physique are apt to sweat more. Therefore, you must adjust yourself through breathing to eliminate agitation and keep calm. After one or two months' practising, you may obtain a consciousness of qi, standing as steady as a stake, as heavy as a mountain and full of vim and vigor.

When doing mid-stance of standing exercise, maintain the foundation of high stance and keep knees further bent, feet apart at the width of three times that of the foot size, gravity sunk, forelegs vertical to the ground and body weight rests at the intersect of the vertical line

through Baihui and Huiyin points with the bottom line between feet heels. Other requirements are the same with high stance of standing exercise (Fig 3—153).

When doing low stance of standing exercise, maintain the foundation of mid-stance and keep knees further bent, feet apart at the width of four times that of the foot size, thighs leveled at 90 degree to the forelegs, knees pointing slightly inward to keep crotch somewhat round and the vertical line through Baihui and Huiyin rests behind the feet. Other requirements are the same with the above (Fig 3—154).

B) The functions of standing exercises in combat.

Long-term practice of continual standing exercise may strengthen one's physique, consolidate body gravity, im-

80

prove muscle-stamina and body balance and thereby help to gain a harmonious strength of the body as a whole. This harmonious strength is released at the moment when touching the opponent's body, which is not only speedy but also explosive with swift variation. Besides, the practice of standing exercise improves one's body sensitivity and combating consciousness.

2. Sitting exercises

It is divided into five positions — regular sitting, crossover sitting, sit-lap sitting, single-lap sitting and double-lap sitting.

A) Regular sitting: Sit regularly on a chair or a stool, keep knees at 90 degree angle, soles put completely on the ground, hands put at the internal sides of the thighs, palms facing up as if holding a body, upper body upright, eyes slightly closed, chin slightly drawn in and tongue touching the palate (Fig 3—155).

Points to remember: when sitting, keep Huiyin point on the edge of the chair or stool, Baihui and Huiyin forming an vertical line, body relaxed and shoulders sunk naturally. Breathe with abdomen style, natural, smooth, deep and soundless. Keep calm both externally and internally against any distraction. Imagine holding two red suns without light in each hand. When feeling warm in palms, imagine with notion that the warmth spreads throughout the whole body and then flows in fits to the Laogong points of the hands and Yongquan points of the

feet. If you suffer any diseases, imagine the *qi* of diseases be discharged through Laogong points and Yongquan points.

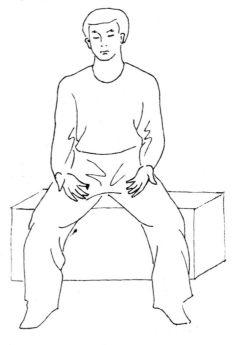

图 3—155

B) crossover sitting

Sit with legs crossover, left foot under the right knee and right foot under the left knee. Put hands on the thighs, palms up. Put the knee as level as possible to the ground. Keep upper body upright, eyes slightly closed, chin slightly drawn in, tongue touching the palate, and Baihui and Huiyin points form a vertical line.

Other requirements and notional activities are the same with Regular sitting.

C) Sit-lap sitting

Sit with upper body upright, left (right) leg put on the ground with knee bent, sole rightward; right (left) leg kept erect with knee bent, sole on the ground and knee under the armpit; palms forming

81

Buddhist greeting in front of the chest; eyes slightly closed, mouth shut naturally, tongue touching the palate. Abdomen-style breathing is adopted (Fig 3—156).

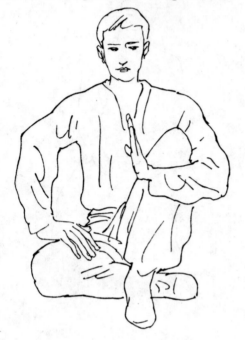

图 3—156

Other requirements and notional activities are the same with Regular sitting.

D) Single-lap sitting

Sit with upper body upright. Keep knees bent and feet overlapped with left foot on the right knee and right foot under the left knee, soles up and toes pointing forward. Put hands on the thighs, palms up. Keep eyes slightly closed, mouth naturally shut, tongue touching the palate and abdomen-style breathing conducted (Fig 3—157a).

Other requirements and notional activities are the same with Regular sitting.

E) Double-lap sitting

Sit with upper body erect. Keep two legs overlapped to each other, knees bent.

Put right foot on the left knee and left foot on the right knee, soles up. Put hands on the thighs, palms up. Keep eyes and mouth naturally closed, tongue touching the palate, shoulders sunk, armpits empty and waist relaxed (Fig 3—157b).

图 3—157a

图 3—157b

82

Requirements and notional activities are the same with Regular sitting.

3. Kneeling exercises

Kneeling exercises are divided into three positions --- double kneeling, double-*kowtow* kneeling and single kneeling.

A) Double kneeling

Part feet shoulder-width apart, toes pointing straight forward. Bend knees to kneel down slowly, shin bones and insteps resting on the ground. Part fingers naturally and press palms on the knees. Keep upper body slightly leaning forward and not sitting on the foot heels. Keep head erect, Baihui point straight upward, shoulders sunk, chest drawn in, waist upright, mouth slightly shut, tongue touching the palate, eyes closed naturally and breathing smoothly and deeply. Imagine with notion that internal *qi* flows into Dantian (Hypogastrium) and forms a mass of *qi* in colour of milk-white. Lead with notion this mass of qi to cycle clockwise for 36 rounds and then anticlockwise for 36 rounds. Concentrate notion on Dantian point (Fig 3—158).

B) Double-*kowtow* kneeling

On the basis of Double kneeling, keep head touching ground, palms put on the ground in front of the head with hollows facing upward, fingers apart, middle and ring fingers pointing to each other respectively, body relaxed, back bent in arc, tongue touching the palate and Hypogastrium slightly drawn in. Other requirements are the same with Double kneeling (Fig 3—159).

C) Single kneeling

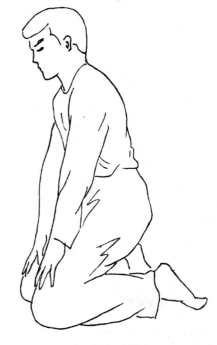

图 3—158

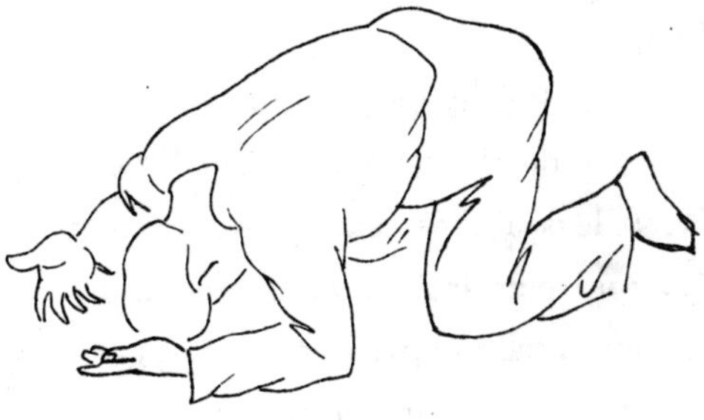

图 3—159

On the basis of Double kneeling, keep left (right) knee bent, foreleg vertical to the ground and thigh level; right (left) leg kneeling on the ground; palm fingers naturally apart with left palm pressing on the left knee and right palm over the left palm. Keep upper body erect, Baihui point leading upward, body weight not resting on the foot heels, eyes and mouth closed naturally and tongue touching the upper palate. Other requirements and notional activities are the same

83

with Double kneeling (Fig 3—160).

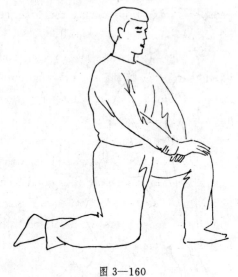

图 3—160

4. Lying exercises

Lying exercises are divided into two positions --- back-lying position and side-lying position.

A) Back-lying position

Lie on the back as normal sleeping. Keep legs abreast and stretched naturally, toes pointing outward; hands put on hipbone, palm downward and fingers naturally bent; head upright, face smiling, eyes and mouth slightly closed, tongue touching upper palate and breathing in abdomen style. Imagine with notion Baihui and Huiyin points are on one straight line through the body, which is hanging in the air and around which there are clouds and mist arising (Fig 3—161).

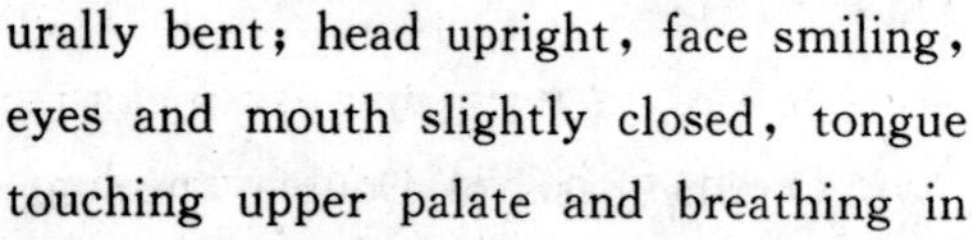

图 3—161

At the beginning of the practice, it is advisable to lie in flat wooden bed without pillows.

B) Side lying position

This includes left and right side lying positions. The following is an example of right side position:

Lie on right side of the body on the bed. Keep legs bent or straight to form a obtuse angle with the body, which looks like a bow; left leg rested on the right leg and right leg on the bed; right palm rested beside the right ear, Laogong point on the palm facing the earhole; left hand rested on the hip; whole body relaxed; eyes and mouth slightly closed and tongue touching the upper palate; breathing in abdomen style. Notional activities are the same with Back lying position (Fig 3—162, 3—163).

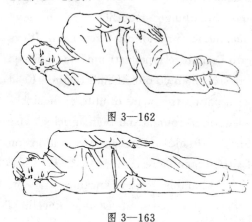

图 3—162

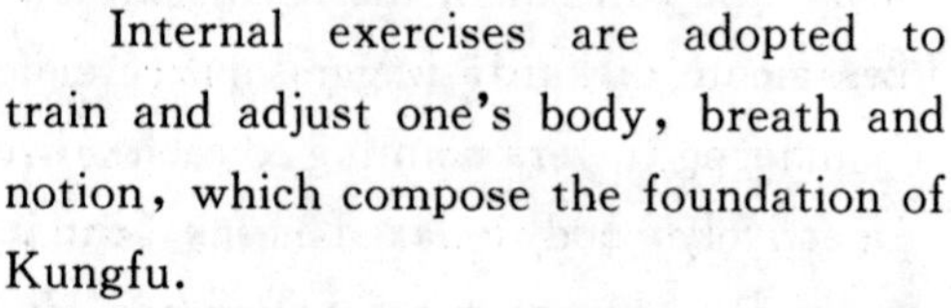

图 3—163

Principles of internal exercises:

Internal exercises are adopted to train and adjust one's body, breath and notion, which compose the foundation of Kungfu.

Relaxing both physically and psychologically is an important link of internal exercises. Relaxing physically is to relax the body and prevent using clumsy and stiff strength. Whenever practising the exercises, position yourself according to requirements and then check your relaxation by notion from the top to the bottom of the body. Check part by part of the body in consequence of head, neck, inner body, outer body and limbs. Make sure there is no stiffness in any part of the body. However, the relaxing does not mean slackness but, rather, making use of notion than strength. Relaxing psychologically is of same importance in that it helps adjust the nervous system so as to relax the body, to obtain good stamina and sensitivity of the muscles and skin, to reduce the resistance of the muscles and increase the speed and explosive strength. In combating, the more relaxed, the more flexible.

One should concentrate one's mind on practice and maintain calm and peaceful, though it is difficult for beginners. Keep practising in compliance with the requirements and you will succeed. To do so, it is helpful to chose a tranquil fresh-aired spot before the practice.

All internal exercises must be natural.

First, breathe naturally. Either normal breathing or abdomen breathing must be smooth and deep without suffocation.

Second, position the body naturally. In any body positions, standing, sitting, kneeling or lying, it is only appropriate to feel comfortable.

Third, be natural in psychological consciousness. Enjoy the practice without reluctance. When having any strange prospects or feelings during the practice, let them come and go naturally.

Besides, it is necessary to keep body upright in order to maintain normal circulation of blood and qi. Clattering teeth slightly helps to get saliva, which is a indication of vitality as is in the case of infant. Swallow the saliva when it is turned out and full in mouth. It does good to inner organs as well as to outer skin. Touch the upper palate with tongue tip to keep calm. Therefore, it is a good habit to clatter teeth slightly and touch upper palate with tongue tip either when training or in daily life.

Follow in order and advance step by step, you will improve your Kungfu without notice.

Section 2　External exercises

Traditional Chinese medicine holds that the tongue relates to heart, eyes to liver, mouth to spleen, nose to lungs, ears to kidneys ··· the five external sensuous organs and the five internal organs are reflective to each other respectively. The health of the internal organs affect the external organs and vice versa. Therefore, none of the Kungfu masters ignores the practice of external exercises while practising internal exercises. In addition to the training of muscles, skeleton and skin, the exercises of the five external organs of mouth, eyes, ears, nose and tongue are also emphasized.

1. Tongue exercising

Tongue is the window of heart and, therefore, tongue exercising is also called heart training, which may be carried out with internal exercises simultaneously. Before starting, get rid of any distracting thoughts and keep calm, adjust breathing to be smooth, deep and soundless. Concentrate at Dantian point. Relax mouth and teeth. Turn tongue around inside the mouth and touch the upper palate with the tip. Clatter teeth slightly, get the saliva and swallow it slowly. The time length of the practice may be decided in accordance with one's health conditions, yet two hours is preferred.

2. Ear exercising

Ears are the windows of kidney and the former will be sensitive if the latter is healthy. When exercising, sit with one leg stretched and the other bent. Relax yourself and get rid of distracting thoughts. Swing your head to both sides for several times. Massage the helixes of ears with thumbs and index fingers for several times. Then, hold out arms straight forward, palms facing forward and fingers up, and turn head to sides in turn for several times according to your feeling appropriate.

3. Eye exercising

Eyes are the windows of the liver as well as the windows of the heart. Whenever awakening from sleep, do not open eyes immediately, instead, with eyes closed naturally, imagine sleeping in the clouds and mist above a vast sea. Massage the eyes with the backs of the index or middle fingers until eyes feel warm. Pause for a moment and move eyes to both sides for several times. Pause again and massage the eye rims with the backs of index fingers for several times and then massage the temples with the index and middle finger. Next, massage the Fengchi points with thumbs and the sides of the nose with index and middle fingers respectively for several times. The purpose of doing this is to have the ears, eyes and nose communicate to each other. Later in a moment, clatter teeth slightly to cause saliva and swallow it slowly. Keep the practice once every morning when awakening for about ten to twenty minutes. When feeling tired at work, do it with standing exercises or sitting exercises accordingly.

4. Mouth exercising

Close mouth and stir the tongue to cause saliva until mouth is full and swallow it slowly. If saliva is inadequate, brush teeth with the tongue and rub the lower and upper gums in turn repeatedly with tongue tip to get more saliva.

5. Nose exercising

Close mouth slightly and breathe with nose. Inhale until chest full and sink the air to the belly by swallowing it. Pause and then draw the belly and chest in forcefully to exhale the air completely through the nose. Make sound as loud as possible by the nose. Do it repeatedly. Massage the sides of nose with index and middle fingers until warm. Close eyes and block the nostrils with middle fingers and push upward for several times. Pull and rub the helixes with index finger and thumb until the ears get warm and red. Swing head to and forth, left and right, and turn head to sides in turn repeatedly. When swinging and turning, keep the body steady. Pause for a minute and hold out arms, fingers pointing up, and push forward from two sides as if closing a gate. Exhale when pushing and inhale when drawing back. The length of the breath should be in accordance with the speed of pushing. Initiate pushing slowly and end it with a sudden, finishing each exhaling simultaneously with the ending of the pushing. Close the exercise after breathing this way with nose repeatedly.

Chapter Two   Ten essential works

Ten Essential Works consist of training of both internal and external work. It is a combination of inheritance of traditional Kungfu and the writer's generalization of his own experience of years which, in turn, has developed and modernized the traditional exercises in terms of methods, facilities and so on. With its concise content and simple facilities, it is easy to learn and effective in use. After a long time of comprehensive training of body shape, muscles and skeleton through the ten essential works, great improvement can be obtained in terms of strength, speed, sensitivity, response, coordination, breath, endurance of attacking, stamina, spirits, and other essentials of Wushu. Besides, it aims also at health and longevity.

1. Head work

A) Baihui hitting

Prepare with a plank of 50cm in length, 4cm in width and 2cm in thickness. Exercise at 5 to 7 in the morning and 5 to 7 in the afternoon, in the sequence of the crown of the head, the forehead, the back of the head and other part of the head.

Stand with feet apart in horse-riding stance or bow stance, toes slightly pointing inward and clutching the ground, looking straight forward and tongue touching the upper palate. Breathe in abdomen style and inhale deeply to sink the

air to Dantian. Pause for a minute and slap the top of the head (Dantian) from light to heavy gradually (Fig 3－164). Utter "hei" when exhale.

图 3－164

When practising at first, slap the head gently until feeling warm, bloated, tingling and painful. Slap heavier gradually until the 4-8cm-thick plank be broken by a single hitting on the head. Then do the next step of training.

B) Ground ramming

Post a handstand with feet abreast, leaning against a wall or a tree. By abdomen breathing, inhale deeply and sink it to Dantian. Pause for a moment and bend arms to ram the ground gently with head (Fig 3－165, 3－166) and exhale simultaneously, uttering "hei". Get *qi* with notion to the top of head. At the first step of training, bend arms slowly and ram gently. Accelerate the bending gradually until being able to take off the hands and let down the body with head ramming the ground (Fig 3 — 167, 3 — 168). When able to do the ramming consecutively for 3 — 6 times, shift to the next exercise.

图 3—165

C) Wall ramming

Facing a wall, stand with feet apart in horse-riding stance or bow stance. By abdomen-breathing, inhale deeply and sink it to Dantian. Pause and then ram the wall with the top, forehead, back and sides of the head, advancing step by step from light to heavy (Fig 3 — 169, 3 — 170), and exhale explosively at the same time. Keep *qi* with notion at the top of

head. Keep practising until able to break bricks or bottles with head.

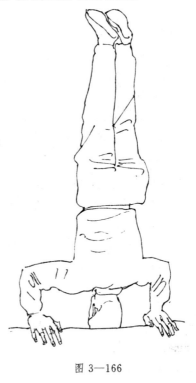

图 3—166

2. Finger and fist work

Prepare with a rectangular plank of 60cm in length, 40cm in width and 4m in thickness. Wrap it with canvas of five to six layers. Fix it on a tripod (wall, tree) at eyebrow high. A sandbag may be used in stead of the plank.

Facing the plank (sand bag) in one arm distance, and stand in horse-riding or bow stance. Breathe with abdomen style. Inhale and simultaneously bend arms slightly to lift the hands upward and forward, palms down, to chest high. Draw right hand back to right chest and left hand to Huagai point of left chest. Meanwhile, get *qi* with notion to Dantian point. Exhale and get four fingers of the

89

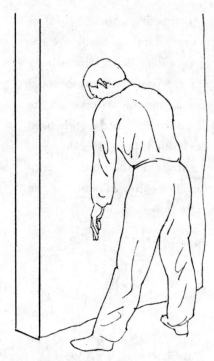

图 3—167

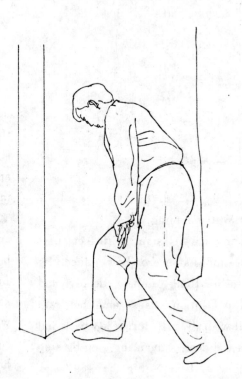

图 3—169

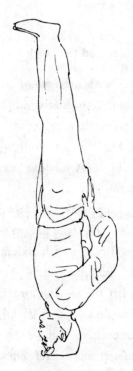

图 3—168

图 3—170

right hand abreast and thrust the palm into the target with force, elbow slightly bent (Fig 3—171, 3—172). Consecutively, without drawing back the hand, clench hand and make a punch with the force of waist twisting and shoulder giving. Look at the right hand (Fig 3—173 3—174).

Practice with left hand in the same way when right hand gets warm, tingling and painful. Finger-fist work is completed in two steps — finger thrusting and hand punching, the latter being the extension and complement of the former. They are usually done in a coherent whole in actual combat. Practising in the morning and evening for half a year will show remarkable effect. With a year's work, one will be able to use the feat at will.

3. Palm striking work

Prepare with a sack of 40cm in length and 30cm in width, filled with 10-20 kilos of greenbeans. Put the sack on a solid stool at crotch high.

Stand arm-length away from the stool in horse-riding stance or bow stance, arms hanging at sides. Breathe in abdomen style. Inhale deeply and sink it to Dantian point. Turn body right and swing right arm in a circle from back to strike the sack with palm downward and fingers pointing forward (Fig 3—175) and exhale simultaneously. Get qi with notion at the palm hollow. Look at right palm.

Consecutively, inhale, twisting waist leftward, and swing right hand from left in a circle, twisting waist rightward, to strike the sack with the back of right palm (Fig 3—176) and exhale simultaneously. Get qi with notion on the handback. Look at right palm. Pressing and cutting can also be used to strike (Fig 3—177, 3—178). Practice with left palm in the same way, from light to heavy, slow to fast, to swing and strike from both sides repeatedly until the palm turns red, hot, tingling and painful. About two months later, the pain will not disappear. When either the palm or the handback can be used to strike objects, proceed to practice cutting. When strong enough, practice with a sack filled with iron grains. Keep practising for a year and the feat can be used in actual combat. One is successful when he is able to break a hanging brick with his handback.

4. Arm work

Prepare with a trunk about 10cm in diameter and fix it upright on the ground. A sand sack may be used for substitution.

Face the trunk in half-arm distance and stand in horse-riding or bow stance. Breathe in abdomen style. Inhale deeply and sink it to Dantian point. Hit the trunk repeatedly with the interior, exterior, front and hind sides of both forearms (Fig 3—179, 3—180, 3—181, 3—182), and exhale at the same time. Get qi with notion to the arms.

When swinging arms, relax the shoulder joints and fingers as possible, but tense the muscles of the arms at the

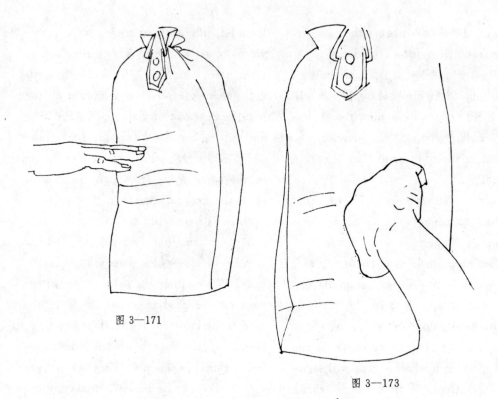

图 3—171

图 3—173

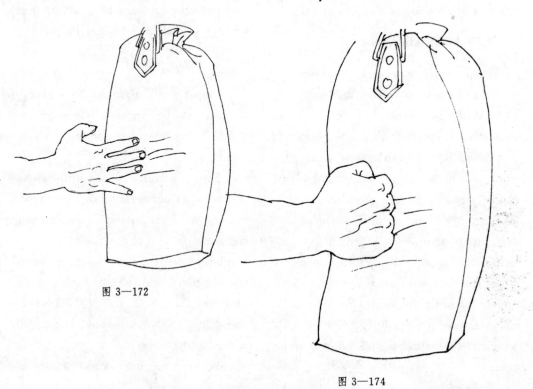

图 3—172

图 3—174

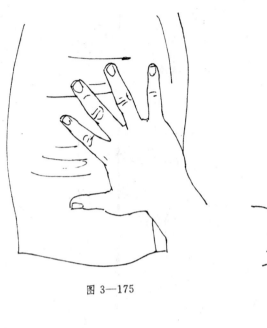

图 3—175

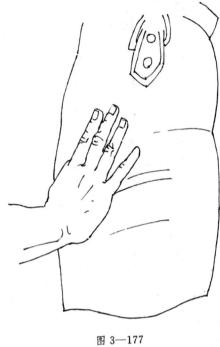

图 3—177

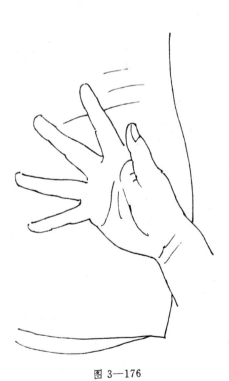

图 3—176

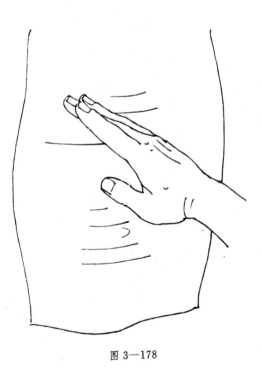

图 3—178

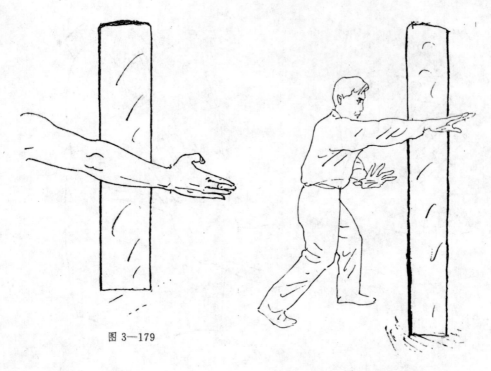

图 3—179

图 3—181

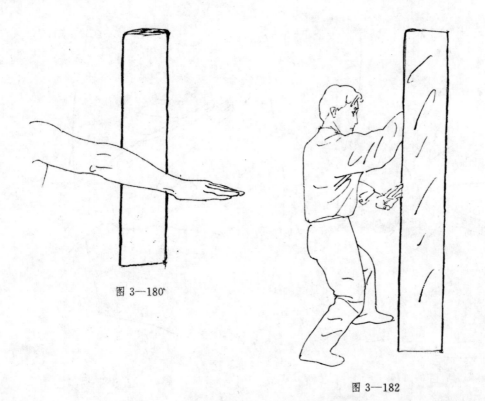

图 3—180

图 3—182

moment hitting the trunk with fingers stretching naturally. Hit the trunk with both arms for eight times while inhaling and exhaling once. Practice from light to heavy, slow to fast, until feeling red, hot and painful of the arms. Use fixed stance at first stage of practice and, having gained certain foundation, shift to Bagua stepping round the trunk. It takes 1 — 2 years to succeed.

5. Elbow work

Prepare a sack filled with 30 kilos of greenbeans or soybeans and hang or set it stable at eyebrow high.

A) Strike the sandsack with elbow

Stand facing the sandsack in horse-riding stance or bow stance. Inhale deeply and sink it to Dantian point. Pause and then turn upper body leftward, slowly lifting arms and bending elbows. Consecutively, turn body rightward, right palm resting on left handback, hollows facing inward, and punch the sand sack with right elbow (Fig 3—183, 3—184, 3 — 185, 3 — 186). Exhale at the same time. Look at right elbow. Get *qi* with notion from Dantian point to the tip of the elbow. Do it with the left elbow in the same way until feeling hot, red and painful with the elbow. Various elbow forms, such as upper-cut elbow, push-elbow and swing-elbow, may be used. Step work can be either fixed or flexible. After training in the way above for three moths to have the strength and coordination of the elbow improved, shift to practice on mat or on the ground.

B) Elbow push-up

Bend elbows, set fists (or palms) in front of shoulders, hollows facing inward, support the body with elbows and front soles of feet, to keep the body above the ground. Set feet abreast, lift head slightly up and look straight forward (Fig 3—187). Breathe in abdomen style. Inhale deeply and sink it to Dantian point. Pause and then move forward with two elbows walking forward (Fig 3 — 188, 3 — 189). Pause and exhale after walking for two steps and then inhale deeply and sink it to Dantian point to go on moving, uttering one, two, three.... You will succeed in elbow work when you are able to move forty-eight steps consecutively with your elbows.

6. Chest and back work

Stand naturally with feet shoulder-width apart. Relax with sunken shoulders and elbows, fingers naturally apart. Breathe in abdomen style. Inhale deeply and sink it to Dantian point. Pause and then lift arms slowly, palms facing downward. Twist waist leftward. Slap left chest with right palm and swing left palm with the waist twisting to slap the back (Fig 3 — 190). Exhale simultaneously, uttering "en", to resist the slapping with the explosion of internal *qi*. Consecutively, twist waist rightward, slap right chest with left palm and swing right palm to slap the back in the same way above (Fig 3—191).

The range and the intensity of the training should be increased gradually, to

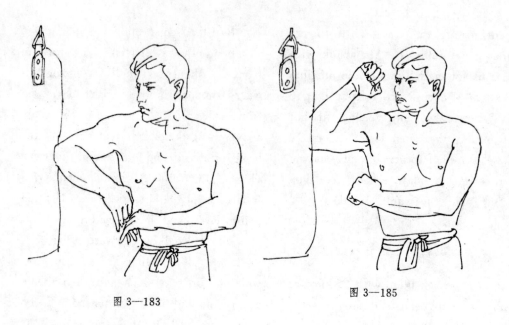

图 3—183

图 3—185

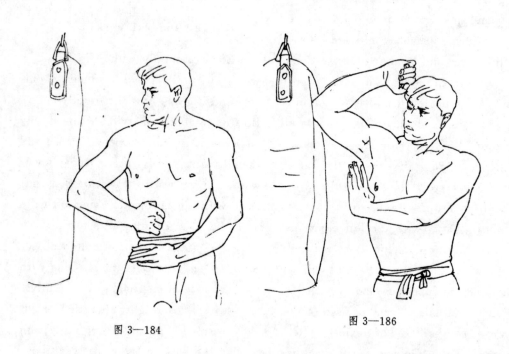

图 3—184

图 3—186

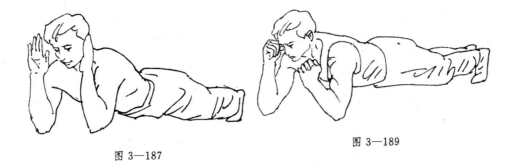

图 3—187

图 3—189

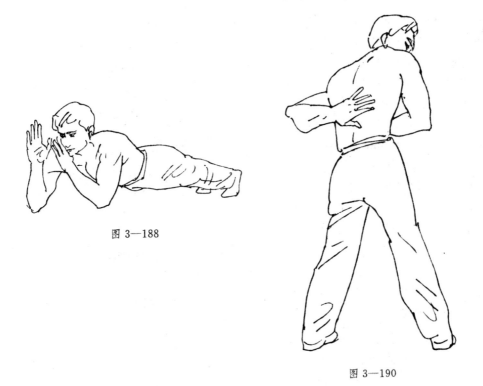

图 3—188

图 3—190

图 3—191

prevent from being hurt. You may also practice with fists, according to your resistant ability. The limitation of slapping is the feeling of being hot, tingling and bloated. After practicing for about six months, the muscles and skeleton of your chest and back become strong with resilience, and a combination of internal *qi* and external strength is formed. Then, slap the chest and back with a plank or bump into the trunk of a tree with body (Fig 3—192, 3—193, 3—194). One is successful in the work when he is able to bump into the trunk two steps away from the tree without being hurt.

7. Chest sides and abdomen work

Stand with feet shoulder-width apart, shoulders and elbows relaxed, arms naturally hung at sides and legs slightly

bent. Breathe in abdomen style. Inhale deeply and sink it to Dantian point. Pause and draw abdomen in vigorously to exhale completely. Pause and then bloat the abdomen. Hit the abdomen and chest sides with two hands (fists or palms) in turn, straining the body and uttering "hei" with internal *qi* to resist the hitting (Fig 3—195, 3—196, 3—197, 3—198). Practise in this way until feeling hot and slightly painful on the chest sides and abdomen. After practising for three months, proceed to hit the chest sides and abdomen with a plank or club. Pause every other minute to breathe normally and renew hitting repeatedly according to the above requirements until sweating all over (Fig 3—199, 3—200). To end the training, breathe deeply for three times. Relax the body and shake or swing the limbs naturally. Finally, massage the abdomen and chest sides with palms for as more times as you like. One will succeed in this work in a year's training.

8. Knee work

Prepare with a sack filled with greenbeans or soybeans.

A) Sandsack-striking with knees

Facing the sandsack hung at abdomen high, stand with feet apart. Breathe in abdomen style. Inhale deeply and sink it to Dantian point. Lift the knee up or sideward to strike the sandsack (Fig 3—201, 3—202) and exhale at the same time. Get *qi* with notion in the knee. Withdraw the knee while inhaling. Practice in this way with right and left

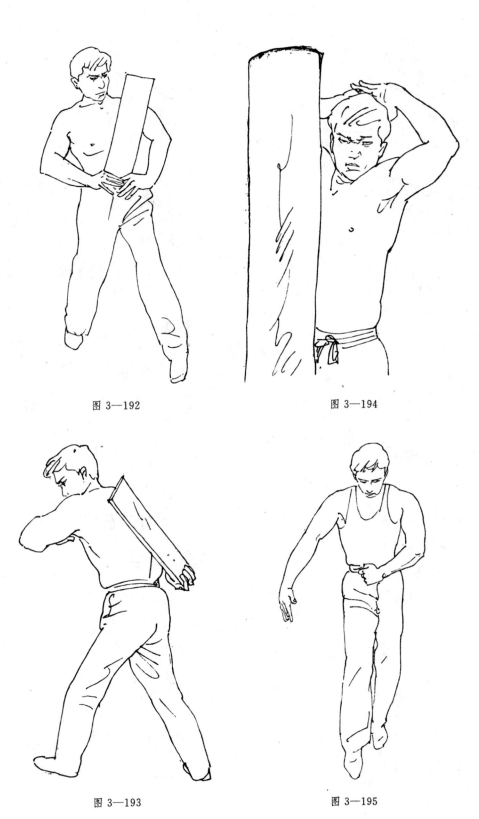

图 3—192

图 3—194

图 3—193

图 3—195

图 3—196

图 3—198

图 3—197

图 3—199

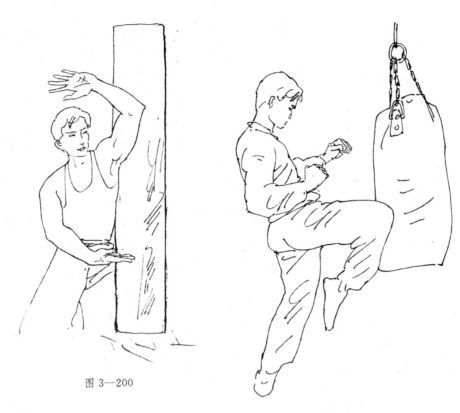

图 3—200

图 3—201

knee in turn repeatedly until feeling hard to bear the pain on the knees.

B) Sandsack-striking by kneeling

Facing the sandsack placed on the ground, stand with feet apart. Breathe in abdomen style. Inhale deeply and sink it to Dantian point. Pause, lifting feet heels, rise on front soles and kneel down to the sandsack (Fig 3 — 203), exhaling simultaneously. Concentrate qi with notion in the knees. Stand up to be ready for next kneel. Practice until feeling hot, tingling and painful with knees. To substitute, practise by kneeling with single knee in the same way. (Fig 3—204)

As knees being strengthened gradually, transfer the practice to jumping-kneeling down to the sandsack.

After training for three months, shift to practice on loose ground in the same way and, six months later, practice on cement or brick pavement. It takes only a year and half to succeed in the work of "iron knees".

9. Foot and leg work

A) Sandsack kicking

Facing a trunk of tree or a sandsack hung at crotch high, stand with feet shoulder-width apart vertically and half a foot-width horizontally, toes pointing forward. Set arms like holding a ball, palms opening naturally. Breathe in abdomen style. Inhale deeply and sink it to Dantian point. Pause and then take hind foot suddenly off ground, body leaning

101

tice in this way until feeling hot, tingling, bloated and painful. Then shift to practice with the other foot.

图 3—202

图 3—204

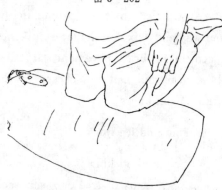

图 3—203

图 3—205

forward, front leg supporting body weight, bend hind knee to lift the leg and kick the sandsack vigorously with front sole of the hind foot, toes backward (Fig 3 — 205). Exhale at the same time and concentrate qi at Yongquan point of the sole. Withdraw the leg and inhale. Prac-

Besides front kicking, practice other feats as follows:

Kick with hind sole of the foot (Fig 3 — 206) with the same essentials as with the front sole; side-kick (Fig 3 — 207), kicking while turning body and concentrating strength on the exterior edge of the foot; and whip-kick (Fig 3—208), kicking while turning body and concentrating strength on the instep.

图 3—206

图 3—207

B) Slabstone kicking

Prepare with a slabstone of 80cm in length, 40cm in width and 10cm in thickness. Lay it half buried in the ground. Face the slabstone and stand with feet vertically apart, front foot a step and half away from the stone. Kick the slabstone in the way of kicking sandsack.

图 3—208

After practice of the above leg work for four months, proceed to practise the work by kicking around the sandsack (trunk or stone). To combine with kicking, other foot work, such as skipping, crossing and jumping, may be adopted. It is advisable to emphasize in practice on the variation of height of legs, position of feet and the force of body turning, waist twisting and crotch sitting in order to make good use of the leg work in actual combat.

10. Post and stake work

Post and stake work is a synthetic practice and improvement of the previous nine works. It is an intensive training of hands, eyes, body, *qi*, strength, sensitivity and flexibility. It simulates actual

103

combat and is of high practical value.

A) Preparation of posts and stakes.

Prepare a post of 2.5m of length and 20cm of diameter (of strong wood such as trunks of date or Chinese scholar tree), strip the peel of it and bury it with 50cm underground. Prepare five stakes of 50cm in length and 10cm in diameter, strip the peel of them and bury them with 40cm under ground (Fig 3—209) and 50cm in radius around the post.

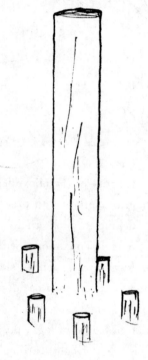

图 3—209

B) Requirements of post and stake work.

It is catalogued into two: fixed-step work and flexible-step work. The former is mainly practiced with fixed stances such as horse-riding stance, bow stance and Kylin stance. The latter, on the basis of the former, is practiced with various step works, striking the stake while moving clockwise or anticlockwise and standing at different height. The practice usually begins with fixed-step work and shift to flexible-step work after practising for a period of time. However, it is difficult for beginners to keep balance and steady steps on the stakes. Therefore, it is advisable not to practice on the stakes at the first stage, but to practice around the five stakes and the post until one is able to walk on the stakes without looking at them and maintain good coordination of the body with step work, smooth breath and solidafied *qi* in Dantian point.

When practising on the stakes, regard the post as the enemy and the five stakes as five positions from which you make attacks toward the enemy. Strike the post swiftly at different height and directions with various feats so as to strengthen the muscle sensitivity, improve actual ability of combating and subtle coordination of attack and defense.

C) The specific training of post and stake work.

This section deals with details of the work, taking the palm work only as the example.

a. Commencing form

Facing the post, stand with feet shoulder-width apart horizontally. Toes forward, arms hung naturally at the sides, fingers abreast (Fig 3—210). Hold palms at the front of the belly, fingers opposing to each other and hollows up (Fig 3—211). Part palms and hold them from sides to the front of the forehead and press downward to the abdomen, fin-

104

gers opposing to each other and hollows down (Fig 3—212, 3—213). Close eyes slightly and concentrate on Dantian point until feeling warm at it and then get on the stakes.

图 3—210

b. Palm practice with fixed step on the stakes

1) Slapping with palms

Facing the post, stand on the two stake with toes pointing forward and clutching down, upper body leaning slightly forward, sink shoulders and elbows and hang arms at the exterior sides of thighs, fingers downward and hollows inward. Look straight forward at the post (Fig 3—214). Stand tranquil for a moment, inhale deeply and sink it to Dantian point. Pause and draw abdomen in to exhale. Simultaneously, turn body rightward, withdraw right palm at left chest,

and lift left palm to slap the post at shoulder level. Look at left palm (Fig 3—215).

图 3—211

Consecutively, withdraw left palm to right chest and, turning body leftward, slap the post with right palm at shoulder level. Look at right palm (Fig 3—216).

2) Slapping with palm backs

Proceed to withdraw right palm to the left chest, turn body slightly right and then left, lift left hand and make a curve via right chest to slap the right side of the post with the handback at eyebrow level. Look at left palm (Fig 3—217).

Consecutively, withdraw left palm to right chest and, turning body slightly leftward and then rightward, lift right hand via left chest to slap the left side of the post with handback at eyebrow level.

图3—212

图3—213

图3—214

图3—215

图3—216

图3—218

图3—217

Look at right palm (Fig 3—218)

3) Up-down hitting and cutting

Following the last movement, withdraw right palm to left chest, hollow inward. Lift left hand before chest and face to hit the post with handback at eyebrow level. Look at left palm (Fig 3—219).

Consecutively, turn body rightward and left palm downward to cut the post with the palm edge at crotch level. Look at left palm (Fig 3 — 220). Proceed to withdraw left palm to chest, hollow inward. lift right hand before chest and face to hit the post with handback at the eyebrow level. Look at right palm (Fig 3 — 221). Next, turn body leftward and right hand downward to cut the post with palm edge at crotch level. Look at right palm (Fig 3—222).

Points to remember: Coordinate striking with breath, inhaling when withdrawing palm and exhaling when strik-

图3—219

图3—221

图3—220

图3—222

ing. Sink the body by slightly bending legs when withdrawing palm, and straighten legs when striking. Two legs perform with equal strength without differentiation of solidness and emptiness. One time practice consists of eight strikings and eight rounds. To close the practice, withdraw both hands, with arms hanging naturally at sides and body relaxed; look at the post and breathe deeply for three times while body straightening slowly; and shift to normal breath and get off the stakes.

c. Palm practice with flexible-step on stakes

For the convenience of exposition, suppose the left-foot stake as stake 1, right-foot stake as stake 2 and the other three as stake 3, stake 4, and stake 5.

Stand on stakes one foot each, lifting arms forward to the shoulder level with palms facing downward. Bend knees to squat slightly, press palms to chest front and sink shoulders and elbows. Withdraw left hand to chest front, turn body slightly left and slap the post with right palm (Fig 3—223).

Consecutively, turn body 180 degree right with left foot stepping rightward onto stake 3, withdraw right palm to the chest front and slap the post with left palm moving in curve. Look at left palm (Fig 3—224). Proceed to turn body 180 degree right with right foot backing onto stake 4 and left foot turning inward to face the post. Simultaneously, slap the post with the right palm at crotch level, making use of the body turning force.

Look at right palm (Fig 3—225).

图3—223

图3—224

109

curve at head level. Look at the right palm (Fig 3—229).

图3—225

Consecutively, withdraw right palm to chest front and slap the post with left palm moving in curve at shoulder level. Look at the left palm (Fig 3—226).

Consecutively, turn body rightward with left foot stepping rightward onto stake 5, back facing the post. Simultaneously, slap the post with left handback at eyebrow level. Look at the left palm (Fig 3—227). Proceed to turn body leftward with right foot stepping forward onto stake 1 and face the post. Simultaneously, withdraw right hand to chest front, slap the post with left palm turning downward with elbow as pivot at ribs level. Look at left palm (Fig 3—228).

Consecutively, twist body leftward, withdraw left palm to chest front and, simultaneously, slap the post with right handback moving in a downward-forward

图3—226

图3—227

110

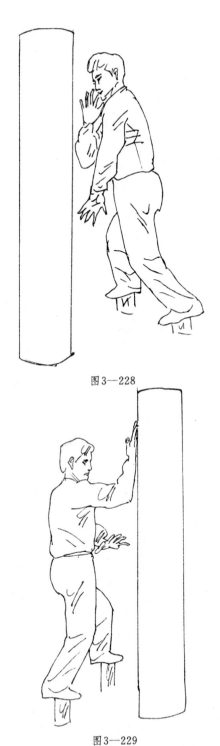

图3—228

图3—229

Consecutively, twist body leftward, withdraw left palm to chest front and turn right hand downward with elbow as

pivot to cut the post with the palm edge. Look at right palm (Fig 3—230).

图3—230

Proceed to withdraw right palm to chest front and slap and then cut the post with left palm (Fig 3—231, 3—232). Finally, close the practice with the same essentials as that of the fixed-step work on stakes. In addition, there are other variables of the practice (Fig 3 — 233, 3—234, 3—235, 3—236, 3—237).

The above palm work of fixed-step and flexible-step on stakes may be practiced interchangeably.

There are a number of other feats in addition to the palm exercises of the post-stake work, such as finger work (Fig 3—238, 3—239), fist work (Fig 3—240), arm work (Fig 3—241, 3—242), elbow work (3—243, 3—244, 3—245, 3—246,

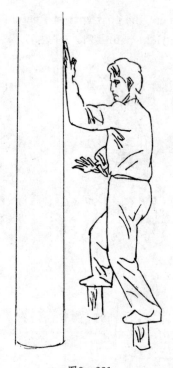

图3—231

图3—233

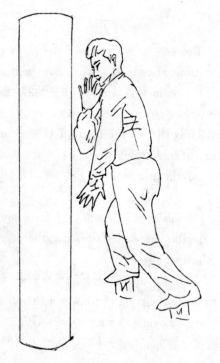

图3—232

图3—234

图 3—235

图 3—237

图 3—236

图 3—238

图3—239

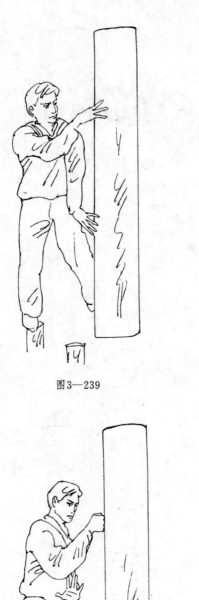

图3—241

图3—240

图3—242

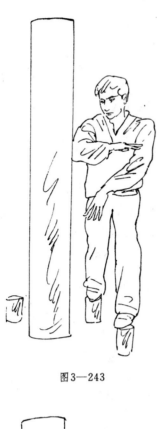

图3—243

图3—245

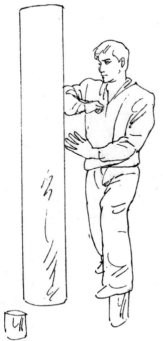

图3—244

图3—246

3—247, 3—248, 3—249, 3—250), chest sides work (Fig 3—251, 3—252), crotch work (Fig 3—253, 3—254), knee work (Fig 3—255), foot work (Fig 3—256), head work (Fig 3—257, 3—258, 3—259, 3—260) and combined work of feet and hands (Fig 3—261, 30—262, 3—263, 3—264, 3—265, 3—266), all of which can be practiced in both fixed-step stake work and flexible-step stake work.

With the basis of the above essential works and the skills of palm work on stakes, keep on practice with the reference of the illustrations. You are sure to achieve mastery of Kungfu through the comprehensive study of the variation of the feats and your combatant competence is bound to be further improved.

Part Four Annexes
Proverbs of Chinese boxing and Kungfu

1. Learning boxing without practising Kungfu is bound to end up in vain; practising Kungfu without learning boxing does not ensure any feats.

2. Boxing practice is aimed at improvement of hands, eyes, body skills and step movements, while Kungfu practice is to strengthen the internal organs.

3. By practising for thousands of times, boxing feats will be accomplished and boundless power will be gained.

4. Internal exercises cultivate one's *qi*, while external exercises temper one's muscles, skeleton and skin. Train your skin in winter and your muscles and skeleton in summer.

5. He who knows only boxing series is incompetent against strength.

He who has only strength is incompetent against Kungfu.

He who has only Kungfu is incompetent against feats.

6. Move the whole body as flexible as a snake, feet steps as fierce as drills, hands as fast as stars and eyes as sensitive as electricity.

7. Practice Kungfu and never stop.

Perform justice and thereby strength grows.

Be externally aggressive and internally reserved.

Think of the major parts and points of the body all the time.

Anticipate the favorable position in combat.

Move fast to attack fast.

Be ruthless to enemy but forgiving to friend.

8. Attack without step work is unskillful whereas step work without attack is useless.

9. When getting close to the component, attack with waist, crotch and elbow; when apart, use feet, knees and hands; when in distance move swiftly to get chances.

10. It is inferior to fight by seizing hair, clutching neck and grasping waist.

11. Be flexible to deal with a stout component who is bigger than you and do not initiate attacks until he does.

Observe by stepping around but never hesitate to attack when chances come.

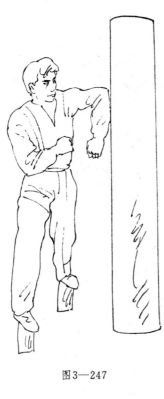

图3—247

图3—249

图3—248

图3—250

图3—251

图3—253

图3—252

图3—254

图3—255

图3—257

图3—256

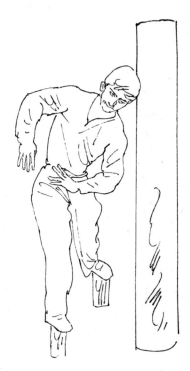

图3—258

图3—259

图3—261

图3—260

图3—262

图3—263

图3—265

图3—264

图3—266

Attack the lower parts of the enemy when you are shorter and be careful to lift your knees.

Keep stepping steady and body low.

Do not raise hand high whereas keep crotch protected.

Stand with feet apart before moving.

Act according to circumstances and be not rash.

Short or tall, it is Kungfu that counts, after all.

12. When acting with upper body., never forget the lower part.and vise versa.

Be sensitive to all directions when moving any way.

13. It is easier to teach boxing than to teach stepping; once the master teaches the disciple how to step, the latter will be superior.

Better give a big sum of money rather than pass feats to others. Nevertheless, offer your feats willingly to one that cherishes benevolence, morality and justice.

14. He who drinks but never gets drunk is noble.

He who restrains himself from sex is a hero.

15. Drinking is a major source of scandal and sex is a energy-cutting sword.

Amity is a magic weapon to maintain longevity while anger is smokeless powder that causes war.

中国拳术与功夫

樊廷强　著

杨大平　译

李兆虬　史琳　绘图

*

中国山东友谊出版社出版发行

（中国山东济南胜利大街 39 号　邮编：250001）

中国山东新华印刷厂印刷

英文版

1998 年 6 月第 1 版　1998 年 6 月第 1 次印刷

ISBN 7—80551—987—0/G · 113

08000